101 WAYS
to strengthen the
PARENT-CHILD
Connection

Devotions, Tips,
& Activities

Michael & Tiffany Ross

An Imprint of Barbour Publishing, Inc.

The authors are represented by and this book is published in association with the literary agency of WordServe Literary Group, Ltd., www.wordserveliterary.com.

Published by goTandem, an imprint of Barbour Publishing, Inc., P.O. Box 719, Uhrichsville, Ohio 44683, www.barbourbooks.com

Our mission is to publish and distribute inspirational products offering exceptional value and biblical encouragement to the masses.

Member of the
Evangelical Christian
Publishers Association

CONTENTS

Part Two: My Trust in God
He Is. . .

Starting Point:
Keys to Unlocking Your Child's Heart

How to Connect and Nurture Spiritual Growth

While we all want childhood to be a carefree time for our kids, the world has become a more dangerous and stressful place. Gone are the days when it was safe for a kid to ride his bike endlessly up and down the street or disappear all day at a friend's house. Tiffany and I cringe when we think about our twelve-year-old son walking home from school alone. While he's a big, tough kid, some bigger threats lurk in our neighborhood.

"Dad, what's a gangster?" he nonchalantly asked us when he was seven.

"Where'd you hear that word?" I asked, my heart skipping a beat.

"At school."

"Was it in a book you're reading—or a story your teacher shared?"

"Nope," Christopher said. "This boy told me his brother is a gangster—and that he's going to be one, too."

I groaned. Here I thought moving from a city to a small town would protect my family from stuff exactly like this.

Remember the days when making the basketball team or the cheerleading squad was among a kid's greatest challenges? But the world in which our son is growing up is filled with more insidious and unpredictable threats: kidnappers, shooters, terrorists, bullies (physical and virtual). . .and, yes, Midwest gangs. Every day he's hit with repulsive messages that bombard him in cyberspace.

For some of his friends, life isn't any better or safer on the home front. Financial uncertainty and joblessness have torn families apart. And there's more, *so much more*: addictions, eroding values, gender confusion, "political correctness," lukewarm faith. . .the list goes on and on. All this stuff chips away at the foundation of civilized society: *the family unit*.

Here's how sociologist Daniel Yankelovich explains our plight:

> *Americans suspect that the nation's economic difficulties are rooted not in technical economic forces (for example, exchange rates or capital formation) but in fundamental moral causes.*
>
> *There exists a deeply intuitive sense that the success of a market-based economy depends on a highly developed social morality—trustworthiness, honesty, concern for future generations, an ethic of service to others, a humane society that takes care of those in need, frugality instead of greed, high standards of quality and concern for community.*
>
> *These economically desirable social values, in turn, are seen as rooted in family values. Thus the link in public thinking between a healthy family and a robust economy, though indirect, is clear and firm.*[1]

Your kids want a deeper connection with you. They need to hear "I love you," "I'm proud of you," and "I won't give up on you."

They need you to be there for them.

Most of all, they need you to guide them into a vibrant faith in Jesus Christ.

Many children are stressed. Many are anxious. Far too many feel constant pressure; now, more than ever, they need change. They long to be accepted by their peers, but most importantly, whether or not they're in a place to admit it, they hunger for family support and connection.[2]

They're counting on you to teach them, protect them, and look after their well-being in this often frightening world. They need you to equip them to navigate life as Christ-followers, secure in their true identity and trusting in the promises of the one true God. My (Michael's) mom did everything possible to shape me into a man who was ready to face the world with confidence. She planted seeds of faith in my life and sparked in me a vision for my future. The influence my mom had on my life was *utterly irreplaceable*—and it's the same in your home.

Here are two key ways a parent influences the lives of their kids:

PARENTS NURTURE THE ABILITIES OF THEIR KIDS

When I was seventeen, Mom bought me a camera. On other occasions, she had given me a typewriter (encouraging the writer in me) and an oil painting set (sparking the artist in me). She seemed to zero in on my talents—then looked for ways to nurture and develop them. Likewise, moms share with their husbands the important role of developing a child's abilities. A parent is both a *coach* and a *mentor*.

A coach teaches, inspires, demands, encourages, pushes, and leads. Good coaches can create great performances in ordinary people. A mentor is a tutor and a model—a person who takes a special interest in the life of another. A mentor possesses the skill to teach and a willingness to do so.

Pause for a moment and think about your child. Who is this kid? What abilities has God given your child? Now think of ways that you can nurture those talents.

Please avoid a common mistake: Keep in mind that nurturing the abilities of your child doesn't mean fitting your child into *your* ideal image of who *you* think he or she should be. Help your child to discover God's will for his or her life, then encourage your child to strive for excellence.

PARENTS PLANT SEEDS OF FAITH

In 2 Timothy 1:5, Paul writes: "I am reminded of your sincere faith, which first lived in your grandmother Lois and in your mother Eunice and, I am persuaded, now lives in you also."

Even though Timothy's mother, Eunice, was Jewish, she had

married a non-Jewish man who was hostile toward the things of the Lord. Timothy's father would not even allow him to be circumcised (Acts 16:1–3). It appears that Eunice shouldered the entire responsibility of raising her son in the faith; she often thanked God for the support of her own mother, Lois. Right from her son's childhood, she made sure that she taught him from God's Word (2 Timothy 3:15), and Timothy ended up becoming a dedicated Jewish man.

Every godly parent is a Eunice to their kids. They set the spiritual tone and provide the example and instruction children need.

That seemingly clueless kid who leaves his dirty socks on the bathroom floor could one day change his generation for Christ (all because he has a God-fearing, praying parent). God is using you to mold your child's character. And whether or not you realize it, your child is tuned in to what you're teaching.

This book can help you maximize every priceless moment together.

HERE'S WHAT YOU'LL FIND ON EACH PAGE. . .

This fast, fun resource is jam-packed with 101 creative ways to help you connect with your kids. . .*and* nurture their spiritual growth. These must-read pages are like three books in one: a daily devotional, a family activity guide, and a parent-child conversation starter. Age-appropriate object lessons bring to life Bible verses about the character and the promises of the Lord, and three key categories guide you through spiritual basics: "My Relationship with God," "My Trust in God," and "My Faith in God." Inside you'll find tips and talking points for. . .

- *Toddlerhood to Preschool*—emphasizing God, Jesus, and the Holy Spirit
- *Kindergarten to Third Grade*—emphasizing God's love, acceptance, and justice
- *Fourth Grade to Seventh Grade*—emphasizing three key issues: self-identity, self-esteem, and acceptance

And each entry offers four creative ways to connect. . .

- *Family Quest*—easy-to-follow activities based on scripture
- *Talk It Out*—questions to get your child talking
- *Parent-Child Connection*—key points to cover and tips on leading a kid-friendly devotional lesson
- *Talk to God*—ideas for how you can pray together

Part One

My Relationship
with God

He Is. . .

1

MY COUNSELOR

The LORD will guide you always; he will satisfy your needs in a sun-scorched land and will strengthen your frame. You will be like a well-watered garden, like a spring whose waters never fail.
ISAIAH 58:11

FAMILY QUEST

Create a safe environment so you and your family can play a fun game of trust. Take turns having one family member wear a blindfold over his eyes so he cannot see his surroundings. Then give him simple instructions to guide him through the room. Tell him things like, "Take three steps forward, feel the wall with your left hand, and take one step to your right." Make sure you give him good instructions to get him across the room safely. Then trade places and let your child guide you across the room while you wear the blindfold. This will build trust.

TALK IT OUT

- Did you like to be blindfolded?
- Did you have a hard time trusting my instructions? Did you think I was going to trick you and make you fall or trip?
- Was it fun to give me instructions? Were you tempted to trick me?
- Do you think God wants to help you make good decisions? How does He help us out?

PARENT-CHILD CONNECTION

Today's activity opens the door for a creative discussion about the Third Person of the Trinity—the Holy Spirit. Help your child understand that He is our Guide, Helper, Strengthener, and Advocate, sent by Christ to live in us and to counsel (or guide) us. Like the Father and the Son, the Holy Spirit is to be believed and obeyed. Say something like this: "In times of trouble—especially those moments when everything and everyone seems very scary—the Holy Spirit of God comes close to you, comforts you, and guides your steps."

TALK TO GOD

As you pray, encourage your child to (1) thank God for always wanting what's best for us and (2) thank Him for the many ways He reaches out to us every day.

2
MY CREATOR

Do you not know? Have you not heard? The LORD is the everlasting God, the Creator of the ends of the earth. He will not grow tired or weary, and his understanding no one can fathom.
ISAIAH 40:28

FAMILY QUEST

Take a look at a globe or a map of the world. Find your hometown and compare its size to that of the whole world. Next, do a Google search and learn how many people live on Earth right now and imagine how many have lived on this planet throughout all time. Each and every one of us has been handmade—each of us is a beautifully unique creation. It's amazing!

TALK IT OUT

- Have you ever seen two people who look exactly the same? Why or why not? (Even twins have differences, right?)
- Next, instruct your child to study his hands, and then say (or read) this: "One-fourth of all your bones are in this part of your body. With them, you can create the most delicate painting or lift heavy weights. And your very own fingerprints are uniquely yours. Now think about your brain. It's so complicated that even the most advanced computer is nowhere near its efficiency. It not only controls your body, but with it you think, you create, you feel, you love, and—along with your spirit—you reach out to God."
- Read Genesis 2:4–25. Point out the important job God gave Adam—naming every living creature (verses 19–20)—and ask your child to spend some time thinking about names of people. Do you think our names help to make us unique individuals? Do

you think God knows the name of everyone who has ever lived? (Answer: Of course He does!)

- Read John 3:16. Based on this verse, how precious are people to God?

PARENT-CHILD CONNECTION

Help your child begin to grasp the wonders of our Creator. Help her see that God is infinitely greater than what our minds can comprehend and that we must approach Him with faith—not courtroom-style facts that skeptics sometimes demand. Emphasize that the God in whom we have come to trust is the *infinite, holy Creator* who has always existed and who made the universe by the power of His word (Hebrews 11:3). Explain that in the Bible (Exodus 3:14) God told Moses, "I AM WHO I AM." Point out that there is only one true God (Isaiah 45:5). He is the sovereign Lord, the God of the Bible, who acts in His creation and who involves Himself intimately in our lives.

TALK TO GOD

As you pray, encourage your child to (1) thank God for creating the world and (2) consider the amazing uniqueness of each human.

3

MY EXAMPLE

Follow God's example,
therefore, as dearly loved children.
EPHESIANS 5:1

FAMILY QUEST

Instruct your kids to draw cartoon panels of Jesus helping others. Encourage them to create a visual story and share it with the whole family. Next, draw another panel that shows how they can help others.

TALK IT OUT

- Do you think Jesus' life was easy? Why or why not?
- How do you know what Jesus was like? Stories in the Bible?
- What does it mean to be Jesus' hands and feet here on earth? (In other words, what does it mean to do what Jesus would do if He were physically here on earth?)

PARENT-CHILD CONNECTION

Emphasize *service*, *giving*, and *kindness*. Explain that Jesus wants us to share God's love with those around us. Ask this question: *"What do people see when they look at your life?"* Explain that others should see "big smiles," nice words, kindness, goodness, friendship—an example that Jesus has set for us! Point out that it makes God sad when we hurt others and use mean words. Obeying parents and elders, and treating friends and family with love and respect, shows that we love God.

TALK TO GOD

As you pray, encourage your child to (1) thank Jesus for being our example and (2) discuss the many ways we can show His love to the world.

4

MY HEAVENLY FATHER

One Lord, one faith, one baptism; one God and Father of all,
who is over all and through all and in all.
Ephesians 4:5–6

FAMILY QUEST

Pull out some photo albums and take a trip down memory lane. Study photos of each family member and note your similarities and differences in appearance. Count how many people live in your house, as well as how many relatives live in other parts of your town, state—even different parts of the world.

TALK IT OUT

- How many of these family members did you choose to live in your house? Any of them?
- Do we get to choose our mother or father?
- Read John 14:15–21. What does Jesus mean when He says, "I will not leave you as orphans" (verse 18)?
- What can we do to remember that we are part of a bigger family—God's family?

PARENT-CHILD CONNECTION

Think about this: If you peer into a telescope and study the heavens, you would no doubt conclude that our Creator is "distant, faraway, and scary" because the universe is dangerous and terrifying. But is this who God is? Absolutely not! It's important that your child knows the truth about this "invisible" Creator we serve, and that the right image is etched into his heart and mind. As you're probably well aware, wrong thoughts about God can cripple even the youngest believer's Christian walk. As our heavenly Father, God is bigger than we can grasp. Yet because of His love, He forgives our sin through Jesus Christ and brings us back into fellowship with Him. Abandoning His unholy, imperfect children is unthinkable to God—just as it was unheard of to the father of the prodigal son.

TALK TO GOD

As you pray, encourage your child to (1) thank Jesus for making us a part of His big family and (2) praise the Lord for His never-ending love.

5

MY FORTRESS

The LORD is my rock, my fortress and my deliverer;
my God is my rock, in whom I take refuge,
my shield and the horn of my salvation, my stronghold.
PSALM 18:2

FAMILY QUEST

Create a "verbal story" together. Tell your child to imagine herself trapped outside in a rainstorm. But then her daddy picks her up and carries her to safety. (Invite your child to fill in the details.) End the story this way: *"He protects you in a warm, dry shelter while the storm passes. He knows what to do and when it is safe to come out."* Now discuss what you both dreamed up.

TALK IT OUT

- Who do you want to be with when you are scared?
- Do you ever pray during those times?
- Do you think that God, your heavenly Father, wants you to ask Him for help?

PARENT-CHILD CONNECTION

Consider reading all of Psalm 91, emphasizing verses 1–2: "Whoever dwells in the shelter of the Most High will rest in the shadow of the Almighty. I will say of the LORD, 'He is my refuge and my fortress, my God, in whom I trust.' " Another great passage to share is Matthew 7:24–27. There are two very important points that you should drive home with today's lesson: (1) God is stronger than anybody or anything in the world; (2) God wants us to call out to Him when we are scared. . .and trust that He will protect us.

TALK TO GOD

As you pray, encourage your child to (1) thank Jesus for always being there for us and (2) ask the Lord to help us pray when we are scared.

6

MY FRIEND

"My command is this: Love each other as I have loved you.
Greater love has no one than this: to lay down one's life for one's friends.
You are my friends if you do what I command."

JOHN 15:12–14

FAMILY QUEST

It's time for a little role-playing. Have your child think of two other kids: one who is a good friend and another who isn't very nice. Now have him pretend to be the kid who is a friend. Your child should use the words and actions they've seen the other kid use. Then have your child switch and imitate the kid who isn't very nice. Discuss which kid shows love. Then ask your child to think about how others might see him. Does he show love?

One word of caution: In order to prevent this exercise from getting out of hand and becoming a "trash-talk fest," set some boundaries. For example, no inappropriate behavior. . .and no brutal comments about the not-so-nice kid.

TALK IT OUT

- Do you have friends? Are some better friends than others?
- Are you a good friend to those around you?
- How is God your friend? How do you know that He is your friend? Do you believe He will ever leave you?

PARENT-CHILD CONNECTION

Since our children's friends can have such a tremendous influence on their lives—especially for tweens and teens—it is crucial that you help them take five key steps: (1) choose friends wisely, (2) evaluate their current friendships, (3) sever bad ties, (4) deflate peer pressure, and (5) build Christian friendships with those who have like-minded values. Share 1 Corinthians 15:33 with your child: "Do not be misled: 'Bad company corrupts good character.' " Translation: Be careful—the kind of people you spend time with will largely determine your life's direction.

TALK TO GOD

As you pray, encourage your child to (1) thank Jesus for making us His hands and feet to the world and (2) ask the Lord for the strength to love those around us—especially those who are hard to love.

1

MY GOD WHO SEES ME

*She gave this name to the L*ORD *who spoke to her: "You are the
God who sees me," for she said, "I have now seen the One who sees me."*
GENESIS 16:13

FAMILY QUEST

Pull out one of those seek-and-find books. Pick one of the puzzles where the objects are hidden in the larger picture (the harder the better). Help your child find the objects listed. You can work several puzzles together if you would like.

TALK IT OUT

- Was it hard to find all of the objects listed?
- Did you know that God cares so much about you that He keeps an eye on you all the time?
- How does that make you feel?

PARENT-CHILD CONNECTION

It's hard to comprehend, but the truth is, God sees each one of us, every second of every day—even among the billions of people who inhabit the planet. Tell your child that God knows us inside and out, and "even the very hairs of [our heads] are all numbered" by God (Matthew 10:30). In fact, He looks right into our minds and knows our thoughts and understands our motives (Psalm 139:2). Help your child to see the Lord's love in His gaze, not His judgment.

TALK TO GOD

As you pray, encourage your child to (1) thank Jesus for caring for us so much and (2) ask the Lord to help us see Him better.

8

MY GUARDIAN

*But the Lord is faithful, and he will
strengthen you and protect you from the evil one.*
2 Thessalonians 3:3

FAMILY QUEST

Ask your child to remember the last time she had a shot. Was it a penicillin shot or an immunization shot for measles, mumps, or some other disease? Talk about what that shot was supposed to guard against or protect her from.

TALK IT OUT

- Have your child indicate some people whose job is to guard and protect us.
- The Bible says that God will protect us from the evil one. Can you think of a time God protected you? (Mom and Dad, this would be a great time for you to share your stories with your kids!)
- What is evil? How does God strengthen you so you can be protected from it?

PARENT-CHILD CONNECTION

Today's focus on "God our guardian" also must involve an honest look at who and what He is guarding us from: Satan and evil. Begin by explaining that the devil is nothing more than an annoying mosquito compared to God's power. Share some biblical clues about Satan's limited power. Read this: "The LORD said to Satan, 'Very well, then, everything he has is in your power, but on the man himself do not lay a finger.' Then Satan went out from the presence of the LORD" (Job 1:12). In other words, the devil operates on a leash that God holds. Next, read Hebrews 2:14 and explain that the fear Satan held over humanity was rendered powerless by Christ. Point out that, as a created being, Satan is not a sovereign, all-powerful being, and he is certainly not equal to God. Because God is all-powerful, Satan does not stand a chance.

TALK TO GOD

As you pray, encourage your child to (1) thank Jesus for the people He provides to keep us safe and pray for those people, and (2) ask Him to guard us in everything we do.

9

MY GUIDE

The LORD will guide you always; he will satisfy your needs in a sun-scorched land and will strengthen your frame. You will be like a well-watered garden, like a spring whose waters never fail.
ISAIAH 58:11

FAMILY QUEST

Save this activity for evening. When it's dark outside, flick off the lights and turn on a flashlight. Have each family member grab someone's hand, and then go for a journey around the house. Carefully navigate your way around furniture, down hallways, up and down stairs—occasionally clicking your flashlight on and off. Eventually arrive at your destination: your bedroom. Climb into bed (assuming it's big enough). Reach into a "treasure bag" (or box) that you placed there earlier, and pull out some snacks, maybe even some drinks. With the lights still out—and the flashlight on—let today's lesson illuminate your minds.

TALK IT OUT

- Begin by reading Isaiah 58:11, followed by this verse: "Your word is a lamp for my feet, a light on my path" (Psalm 119:105).
- How did this flashlight help us get to our destination? What happened when I turned off the light?
- In the same way, God's Word—the Bible—is like a torch or a lamp on a dark night. Can you think of ways that it lights our path in life? (Solicit answers like, "It prevents us from stumbling into bad choices," and "Through it God guides us onto the right paths.")
- How do God and His Word guide us to heaven?

PARENT-CHILD CONNECTION

Explain that even though God has promised to guide us, He will never force us to do the right thing. Read Psalm 46:10—"Be still, and know that I am God"—and point out that the Lord wants us to trust Him and obey His instructions. And if we do, He will illuminate our path and lead us in the right direction. But emphasize that God has given us free will. He will not make choices for us. Faith involves obedience—taking that step in the right direction and freely choosing to follow Jesus. . .day by day, choice by choice.

TALK TO GOD

As you pray, encourage your child to (1) thank Jesus for His amazing love for us and (2) ask the Lord for His guidance every day.

10

MY HEALER

*Heal me, LORD, and I will be healed; save me
and I will be saved, for you are the one I praise.*
JEREMIAH 17:14

FAMILY QUEST

Have your child pick out his or her favorite doll or action figure. Join with your child as you both make up a big adventure for the toy. During the adventure, have your child be the toy's protector. When danger threatens, have your child help the toy escape. Throw a big celebration when the toy arrives home safely. Now you can explain that this is the way God looks out for us.

TALK IT OUT

- Do you ask God for help when you are hurt?
- Does God enjoy taking care of you?
- Does God heal only our bodies? Does He heal our hearts, too?

PARENT-CHILD CONNECTION

Share the Gospel during today's lesson. Explain that each of us has a condition inside that can separate us from God. It's called sin. But we have the one and only cure, too: forgiveness and salvation through Jesus Christ. Read Mark 1:40–45, and then say this: "When the Great Physician reached out His hand and said, 'I am willing,' He was also talking to you and me. When that pitiful, struggling, dying man made his way to see the Holy One and said, 'You can make me clean,' how did Jesus respond? Was He grossed out? No. He did what only a Savior would do. He stretched out His hand and healed. He also stretches out His hand to you and me today. He loves us in spite of our sin. He wants to forgive us and cure us of our deadly disease—the disease of sin. 'I am willing,' He says. 'Are you?' "

TALK TO GOD

As you pray, encourage your child to (1) thank Jesus for good health and comfort when we are sick and (2) ask the Lord to take special care of your family.

11

MY HELPER

*"For I am the LORD your God who takes hold of your
right hand and says to you, Do not fear; I will help you."*
ISAIAH 41:13

FAMILY QUEST

We have built a lot of safety nets into our society. Describe a simple but serious situation to your child and ask whom he would call. For example, if there is an emergency, your child would call 911. If he has a bad dream at night, he would call for Mom or Dad. At the end of your list, ask one final question: When do you call for God?

TALK IT OUT

- How do you call God for help?
- Does He always answer us the way we want Him to?
- Read Proverbs 15:29. Can we trust that God hears our prayers? (Why or why not?) How many times can we ask Him for help?

PARENT-CHILD CONNECTION

When your child takes a tumble or is picked on by other kids, you instinctively come to the rescue: "It hurts right now, but I'll fix you up with a bandage and a kiss. You'll be as good as new!" Similarly, when we as God's children take a spiritual tumble, He is right there to pick us up and soothe our wounds. God does this because He is our Father and our Helper, and He knows exactly what we need. . .and the precise moment that we need it. Take the opportunity to drive home these truths. Model for your kids the habit of "praying first and seeking God's help when life is hard." Teach them that Jesus cares about every detail of our lives. He suffers what we suffer and feels what we feel. He came to be our friend. "Peace I leave with you; my peace I give you. I do not give to you as the world gives. Do not let your hearts be troubled and do not be afraid" (John 14:27).

TALK TO GOD

As you pray, encourage your child to (1) thank Jesus for hearing his prayers and (2) ask the Lord to show your family how to pray during times of need.

12
MY HOPE

May the God of hope fill you with all joy and peace as you trust in him,
so that you may overflow with hope by the power of the Holy Spirit.
ROMANS 15:13

FAMILY QUEST

Discuss the future. Take turns listing ideas and events you are looking forward to. Include whether or not you think your plans for the future will come true.

TALK IT OUT

- Read Romans 15:1–4. What does this passage say about hope?
- Is God part of your future plans?
- How can God be the source of your hope?

PARENT-CHILD CONNECTION

As Christians, our hope should be anchored in a growing relationship with Jesus—not in how much money we have, how many "toys" we've amassed, or how popular we are. Spend some time talking to your child about the essence of true success, real happiness, and lasting hope. Explain that success in God's eyes means giving up everything for Him. . .in order to gain what He has in store for us. It's sometimes true that in doing so some believers may never achieve what they always dreamed they'd become. However, when we fully surrender our lives to God, He often returns those dreams and talents in bigger, grander ways than we could ever imagine. Knowing, serving, and following Jesus are the keys to success. . .and the foundation of lasting hope.

TALK TO GOD

As you pray, encourage your child to (1) thank Jesus for being in control of our future and (2) express to the Lord her own hopes and desires for the future.

13

MY JUDGE

*This will take place on the day when God judges
people's secrets through Jesus Christ, as my gospel declares.*
ROMANS 2:16

FAMILY QUEST

Turn your living room into a courtroom, and take turns sitting on the "judge's seat." This activity involves four roles: (1) *defendant*—the person accused of breaking "family law"; (2) *prosecuting attorney*—the person who reads a list of charges against the defendant and argues for a "guilty" verdict; (3) *advocate*—the person who defends the accused and argues for a "not guilty" verdict; and (4) *judge*—the person who weighs the evidence and decides if the defendant is guilty or not guilty of breaking family law. Before the trial begins, write out several lists of wacky charges—for example, "The accused belches loudly during dinner, chases the cat, bugs their siblings, combs their hair to the left instead of to the right, rewears smelly socks"—and place the lists in a large bowl. Once you've assigned the parts and taken your positions, instruct the prosecuting attorney to randomly pull out a list of charges and begin the courtroom drama. Ham it up, be creative, ad-lib. . .even use crazy accents and voices with each part you play. Once everyone has had a chance to be the judge, open your Bible and read these verses: Romans 2:16; 8:1–4; and Ephesians 1:7.

TALK IT OUT

- During our crazy trial, who decided the *right* and *wrong* way of acting or looking? Was it fair?
- The Bible tells us that we are all guilty of breaking the law—God's law—and that we will have our day in court. We will all stand before the ultimate Judge. Yet through Jesus, we are found

"not guilty" and are completely forgiven. How does this make you feel?

- How are we set free through Jesus? (Hint: Find the answer in Romans 8:1–4.)
- How can we be confident of our forgiveness? (Hint: Find the answer in Ephesians 1:7.)

PARENT-CHILD CONNECTION

Teach three important concepts: (1) *We must accept God's forgiveness.* When we've blown it in some way, we must go to the Lord in prayer, confess our sin, ask for forgiveness, and press ahead with the power of the Lord. (2) *We must learn from our mistakes.* It's every Christian's responsibility to practice avoiding the traps that cause him or her to stumble. (3) *We must submit to God's instructions.* Keep in mind that God isn't finished with us; the paint is still wet and our faith is still under construction. Growing up in the Lord is a lifetime process. We'd be wise to listen to His instructions and do our best to obey them.

TALK TO GOD

As you pray, encourage your child to (1) thank Jesus for His fairness and love and (2) ask the Lord to help him always remember that God is the final judge of everything.

14

MY KING OF KINGS

On his robe and on his thigh he has this name written:
KING OF KINGS AND LORD OF LORDS.
REVELATION 19:16

FAMILY QUEST

Today's activity is especially suited for young children. Using gold-colored poster board or purple and yellow construction paper, help them create a "King of Kings" crown. Encourage them to color it and then decorate the royal headpiece with sequins, glitter, and other shiny treasures. In addition to the crown, help them make hats for a cast of other characters in your make-believe castle: a queen, a prince and a princess, brave knights, even a crazy court jester. Next, pick a chair that will serve as your throne, and gather some old coats and shawls that the kids can use as robes and formal wear. When the stage is set, have everyone pull on a costume and take part in a magical celebration. Let them take turns ruling the party as king. End with a reading. Have everyone sit quietly on the floor and listen as you share Revelation 22:1–5. (We recommend using *The Message*.)

TALK IT OUT

- The Bible verses I just read give us a beautiful picture of our King and His kingdom. What will it be like to see His face?
- What does a king do? How important is it that a king is good?
- How can God be your King?
- What do you think the ultimate kingdom—heaven—will be like?

PARENT-CHILD CONNECTION

The point of today's activity and lesson is to help your child understand the lordship of Jesus Christ and to begin seeing Him as the King of kings. It's also designed to help a young heart grasp that heaven is a real place—the ultimate kingdom; our destination as Christians. It's the eternal garden where we will walk with Him "in the cool of the day" (Genesis 3:8) and "be like him, for we shall see him as he is" (1 John 3:2). It will be a place without fear or shame, a place without pain, suffering, hatred. . .or regret. Just perfect harmony. Point out that getting to heaven is not about how good we are or how many good deeds we do. The only way we can someday live there "forever and ever" is to be friends with Jesus Christ. This means believing that He is our Lord and Savior and then asking Him to live in our hearts and to be the King of our lives. If you haven't yet done so, invite your child to give her heart to Jesus. End today's lesson in prayer.

TALK TO GOD

As you pray, encourage your child to (1) thank God for being our King and Lord and (2) ask Him to help us honor Him with respect and love.

15

MY LORD

For the LORD is our judge, the LORD is our lawgiver,
the LORD is our king; it is he who will save us.
ISAIAH 33:22

FAMILY QUEST

Have your child create a short skit. He needs to come up with characters, location, props, and dialogue. Then it's up to *you* to act out every word and action under his direction. Now compare the role of the creator of the skit to God who created us. As our Creator, He is also our director.

TALK IT OUT

- What does the name *Lord* mean?
- Do we have to do what God wants or do we have a choice?
- Does God always know best?

PARENT-CHILD CONNECTION

As Christians, we believe that Jesus is the ruler and guide of our lives, so we refer to Him as our *Lord*. In other words, we do our best to submit wholly to Him and to obey His commandments in the Bible, as well as the promptings of the Holy Spirit. Here's how you can explain this concept to a child: Point out that we view Jesus as our absolute authority and so we must obey Him the same way that a child must obey his parents. Yet Christ is the authority of our lives *because He is the author of existence*. He isn't just our boss or our master; He is our maker. The Bible tells us that the Son of God created all things and that in Him all things are held together (Nehemiah 9:6; Colossians 1:17). Grasping this truth will change the way your family will see His commandments and

His teachings. Christ's decrees are much more than the law of the land; they represent the laws of physics.[1] If they tell us how to act, it's because they first tell us how things are designed to work.[2] Jesus Himself is truth, and for this reason, trusting His lordship is the only way to experience life as it really is and should be. In Him "we live and move and have our being" (Acts 17:28).

TALK TO GOD

As you pray, encourage your child to (1) thank Jesus for being Lord of all who believe in Him and (2) tell the Lord how sorry he is for sometimes doing things that disappoint God.

16

MY ONE TRUE GOD

*"Now this is eternal life: that they know you,
the only true God, and Jesus Christ, whom you have sent."*
JOHN 17:3

FAMILY QUEST

Grab a marker, tape a piece of white construction paper to your wall, and take turns listing all the different names we have for God. Here are a few to get you started: He is the Shepherd who guides (Genesis 48:15), the Lord who provides (Genesis 22:8), the Lord of peace during life's trials (Judges 6:24), the Physician who heals the sick (Exodus 15:26), and the Banner that guides the soldier (Exodus 17:8–16). Add many more names to your list, and discuss how amazing it is that in spite of all the different ways we can describe our amazing Creator, they each refer to our one true God!

TALK IT OUT

- What is your favorite name for God?
- Are there any names that you don't understand?
- Why are there so many names?

PARENT-CHILD CONNECTION

As you explore the many names of God, weave into the discussion three important faith issues that your child needs to learn: (1) *Even though there is only one true God, He is triune.* There are within the Godhead three persons—the Father, the Son, and the Holy Spirit. (2) *The work of salvation is one in which all three act together.* The Father freely gives us redemption, the Son secures it, and the Spirit applies it. (3)

The New Testament warns us to beware of misguided people who deny that Jesus Christ is the only way to eternal life. "I am astonished that you are so quickly deserting the one who called you to live in the grace of Christ and are turning to a different gospel—which is really no gospel at all. Evidently some people are throwing you into confusion and are trying to pervert the gospel of Christ" (Galatians 1:6–7).

TALK TO GOD

As you pray, encourage your child to (1) thank Jesus for reaching out to us in so many different ways and (2) ask the Lord to help us understand all the things these names tell us about God.

17

MY PHYSICIAN

Some time later, Jesus went up to Jerusalem for one of the Jewish festivals. Now there is in Jerusalem near the Sheep Gate a pool, which in Aramaic is called Bethesda and which is surrounded by the five covered colonnades. Here a great number of disabled people used to lie—the blind, the lame, the paralyzed. One who was there had been an invalid for thirty-eight years. When Jesus saw him lying there and learned that he had been in this condition for a long time, he asked him, "Do you want to get well?" "Sir," the invalid replied, "I have no one to help me into the pool when the water is stirred. While I am trying to get in, someone else goes down ahead of me." Then Jesus said to him, "Get up! Pick up your mat and walk." At once the man was cured; he picked up his mat and walked.

JOHN 5:1–9

FAMILY QUEST

Buy or rent the DVD *The Gospel of John* (Buena Vista Home Entertainment / Disney, 2005), and show scenes from John 5:1–15 and John 9:1–41—re-creations of Jesus healing those who were blind, lame, or paralyzed. Pass out popcorn and sodas and make it a movie night. When you're finished watching these powerful chapters from the book of John, talk about Christ's healing power—specifically, how He is *our* Great Physician, too.

TALK IT OUT

- How do you think the man who had been disabled for thirty-eight years felt? (See John 5:5–6.) Why did Jesus ask, "Do you want to get well?"
- In what ways does the Great Physician begin to stitch our wounded lives back together again? What kinds of things

prevent us from being healed?

- Describe the wounds and ailments—physical and spiritual—that you need Jesus to treat in your life.
- How's your own spiritual sight? Is it "20/20"—sharp, healthy, and well developed? Are you nearsighted (a bit selfish) or farsighted (taking your eyes off of Jesus)? What steps can you take to correct your vision?

PARENT-CHILD CONNECTION

All who commit their lives to Jesus receive *salvation* (eternal life), *liberation* (freedom for the captives) and *restoration* (healing of the brokenhearted). Focus on that third point today. Explain that yes, indeed, Christ is still at work in the world, healing those who are blind, lame, and paralyzed. And He is transforming those with broken hearts and giving sight to the spiritually blind. One of the key ways that the Great Physician touches our lives is through His Word. When His truths are worked into our lives consistently, God speaks to us intimately and guides us in unique ways. There is a supernatural component to the Bible that no one can explain. It has to be experienced. And the more we engage the scriptures—and respond to what God says—the more our lives are molded into what He wants them to be. God's Word gets past our heads, touches our hearts, and revives our souls.

TALK TO GOD

As you pray, encourage your child to (1) thank Jesus for good health and comfort when we are sick and (2) ask the Lord to take special care of her family.

18

MY REDEEMER

You came near when I called you, and you said,
"Do not fear." You, Lord, took up my case; you redeemed my life.
LAMENTATIONS 3:57–58

FAMILY QUEST

Watch a movie with your kids: *The Chronicles of Narnia: The Lion, the Witch, and the Wardrobe* (Walt Disney Pictures / Walden Media, 2005). Afterward, sit in a circle and recap what happened to the young character named Edmund Pevensie: He betrayed his siblings to the White Witch while under her evil influence. But as the story progressed, he owned up to his shortcomings and admitted the error of his ways. Edmund was even redeemed by the intervention of Aslan, and the boy eventually joined the battle against the witch. But what price did "the Great Lion" have to pay for Edmund's freedom? Aslan agreed to lay down his life on the Stone Table! Was Aslan gone forever? Did the evil witch win? Of course not! The Great Lion's sacrifice saved not only Edmund but all of Narnia as well. Now tie in the story with an activity your child can relate to. Say something like this: "Have you ever played a video game where you were cast into a prison cell and had to have a certain number of tokens to buy your release? Could you get out of your predicament any other way? If you didn't have the needed tokens, what happened to you?" Spend the remainder of your devotional time connecting make-believe worlds with reality. . . .

TALK IT OUT

- In real life, Someone did the same thing for us. His name, of course, is Jesus Christ. What did Jesus "redeem" for us?
- How did He do it?
- What would have happened to us had He not redeemed us?

PARENT-CHILD CONNECTION

During today's lesson, define the word *redeemer* this way: "someone who obtains the release or restoration of another from captivity by paying a ransom; someone who delivers another from sin and its consequences by means of a sacrifice offered for the sinner." What a perfect description of Jesus Christ and what He did for us! Take the opportunity to share very clearly how Jesus has redeemed each one of us:

- All of us have sinned and fall short of God's holiness (Romans 3:23).
- The result of unforgiven sin is death. But God's gift is eternal life given to us by Jesus Christ our Lord (Romans 6:23).
- Jesus is the only One who can bring us to God (1 Timothy 2:5).
- Even though we are guilty of sin and deserve death, God loved the people of this world so much that He gave His only Son, so that everyone who has faith in Him will have eternal life and never die (John 3:16).
- Jesus died on the cross for us, paying the price for our sins (Philippians 2:8).
- Jesus rose from the dead on the third day, defeating death and giving eternal life to all who will believe in Him (1 Corinthians 15:3–5, 20–22).
- You will be saved if you honestly say, "Jesus is Lord," and if you believe with all your heart that God raised Him from death. God will accept you and save you if you truly believe this (Romans 10:9–10).

TALK TO GOD

As you pray, encourage your child to (1) thank Jesus for being willing to redeem her and (2) ask the Lord to show her ways to serve the One who redeemed her.

19

MY ROCK

He is the Rock, his works are perfect, and all his ways are just.
A faithful God who does no wrong, upright and just is he.
DEUTERONOMY 32:4

FAMILY QUEST

Gather some rocks from your yard. Examine them together and discuss their characteristics.

TALK IT OUT

- What are some things that are made of rock? (Mountains, statues, pyramids.)
- How long do you think it would take for a rock to change?
- How can God be your rock?
- Does this change your image of God?

PARENT-CHILD CONNECTION

Emphasize the importance of building our lives on the solid rock of Christ's teachings in the Bible. Read the parable about the wise and foolish builders: "Therefore everyone who hears these words of mine and puts them into practice is like a wise man who built his house on the rock. The rain came down, the streams rose, and the winds blew and beat against that house; yet it did not fall, because it had its foundation on the rock. But everyone who hears these words of mine and does not put them into practice is like a foolish man who built his house on sand. The rain came down, the streams rose, and the winds blew and beat against that house, and it fell with a great crash" (Matthew 7:24–27).

TALK TO GOD

As you pray, encourage your child to (1) praise God that He is perfect and strong, and (2) thank Jesus for His faithfulness.

20
MY SAVIOR

"Salvation is found in no one else, for there is no other name under heaven given to mankind by which we must be saved."

ACTS 4:12

FAMILY QUEST

Hand out a photocopy of a challenging but kid-friendly maze. (You can pick up a collection of fun mazes online at Amazon or Walmart, as well as at most bookstores.) Instruct everyone to work the puzzle with a pen (not a pencil) so all of the mistakes can be seen. Afterward, take a look at each other's papers—mistakes and all. Compare this to our journey in life. Each day can bring its share of challenges and confusing choices, and we all end up making mistakes from time to time. But in the end, there is only one true path to God—through His Son, Jesus Christ. We need a Savior.

TALK IT OUT

- Do you think everyone wants to know God?
- What are some of the ways people try to figure out who God is?
- Do you believe that Jesus is the only path to God? Why or why not?

PARENT-CHILD CONNECTION

Explain that there's a spiritual tug-of-war going on in each of our hearts that can knock us off course. On one hand, we want to do what's right. We want to obey what the Bible tells us, and we desire to know Jesus better. But sometimes we make bad choices and don't fully understand why we messed up—especially when we are tempted by something. The apostle Paul knew this all too well: "I do not understand what I do. For what I want to do I do not do, but what I hate I do" (Romans 7:15). Paul learned that the tug-of-war is sin working in us. We all need help—a savior—to guide us and to help us live right. The good news is, we have one: Jesus Christ! Believe it or not, if we surrender the internal fight to Him, our Savior will help us through the maze of bad choices and will give us the strength to follow Him. But it's up to us to call on our Savior. We can choose life by the Spirit and work into our hearts the qualities of God: love, joy, peace, patience, kindness, goodness, faithfulness, gentleness, self-control. Or we can choose the acts of the sinful nature and allow ourselves to degenerate with the cravings of the flesh: sexual immorality, impurity, debauchery, idolatry, hatred, discord, jealousy, fits of rage, selfish ambition, dissensions, factions, envy, drunkenness (see Galatians 5:16–26). The right path is the one laid out for us by our Savior.

TALK TO GOD

As you pray, encourage your child to (1) thank Jesus for being our Lord and Savior and (2) ask the Lord to keep us on the "path of truth."

21
MY SHEPHERD

The LORD is my shepherd, I lack nothing. He makes me lie down
in green pastures, he leads me beside quiet waters, he refreshes my soul.
He guides me along the right paths for his name's sake.

PSALM 23:1–3

FAMILY QUEST

Find a quiet place to lie down and read today's scripture passage. Then grab some colored pencils and draw what you pictured when you read these verses. Have your child do the same. Compare your pictures.

TALK IT OUT

- How does this passage make you feel?
- Discuss what "green pastures," "quiet waters," and "right paths" mean to you.
- In what ways does a shepherd care for his sheep? How is God your shepherd?

PARENT-CHILD CONNECTION

Scripture beautifully depicts Christ's deep love and total commitment to us through the depictions of Him as our shepherd. Read John 10:1–21, emphasizing verses 14–15: "I am the good shepherd; I know my sheep and my sheep know me—just as the Father knows me and I know the Father—and I lay down my life for the sheep." Explain that the life of a dedicated shepherd means total devotion to his flock—a devotion that includes putting the lives of the sheep above his own. First of all, there are thieves and robbers—dishonest men who try to lure stray lambs away from the flock and steal them. Second, there are plenty of wild animals—mostly wolves. Whenever they close in, fierce and ravenous from hunger, the hired hands usually split. Why should they risk their lives for somebody else's property? But the committed shepherd never looks upon his flock as "property." He's grown to know and love each of the sheep as individuals. In fact, his love and dedication to them are so intense that he would actually fight to the death to protect them. Jesus is the Good Shepherd for us.[1]

TALK TO GOD

As you pray, encourage your child to (1) thank Jesus for taking care of him and (2) ask the Lord to help him live for Jesus.

22
MY SHIELD

The LORD is my strength and my shield;
my heart trusts in him, and he helps me.
My heart leaps for joy, and with my song I praise him.
PSALM 28:7

FAMILY QUEST

Gather some construction paper, scissors, and colored pencils. Create a shield with the paper and decorate it with symbols of God such as the cross, a dove, a flame of fire, a lamb, and the symbols for alpha and omega.

TALK IT OUT

- What are shields used for?
- How is God your shield?
- Explain the symbols you drew on your shield.

PARENT-CHILD CONNECTION

During today's lesson, emphasize that Jesus is our shield (Psalm 84:11) and our faith (Galatians 2:20). A Christian's armor is nothing more, and nothing less, than a multifaceted presentation of who Jesus is to us. If we need protection from the temptation to lie or to steal, we need more of Jesus. In all honesty, that's the upside of any temptation. The things that tempt us to sin can also end up motivating us to depend more on Jesus, allowing Him to be our shield. And when those burning darts start flying—*I could so easily slip that candy in my pocket without anyone seeing me*—you can raise your shield with a simple prayer: "Jesus, I need You!" Keep holding up the shield until those smoldering arrows get extinguished.

TALK TO GOD

As you pray, encourage your child to (1) thank Jesus for being her shield and (2) ask the Lord for joy in her heart and help to always trust Him.

23

MY SOURCE

The Son is the radiance of God's glory and the exact representation of his being, sustaining all things by his powerful word.
HEBREWS 1:3

FAMILY QUEST

Plug in a radio, a clock, and a lamp and position them on a table. Next, place a glass of water, some healthy snacks, and a Bible on the table. Say this: "Many things in this world are powered by electricity, but people are fueled by food and water. And in order to grow spiritually, we need God's Word." One by one, unplug the appliances. Now talk about how Christians stay plugged into our "Power Source": God.

TALK IT OUT

- What happened when I unplugged the appliances?
- What would happen to us if we didn't eat food or drink water?
- Now think about our relationship with Jesus. What would happen if we stopped praying and reading the Bible?

PARENT-CHILD CONNECTION

Following Jesus and growing closer to Him is an interactive experience. "Come near to God and he will come near to you" (James 4:8). It's both private and public. It involves our heart (prayer, worship) and our head (Bible study, church attendance). And as we linger in God's presence—praising Him or closing our eyes and mouths and just being still before Him—it's as if we get a high-voltage spiritual zap. Prayer, worship, and Bible study build us into stronger Christians. Help your child understand that during our devotional times with God, we *should*

(1) give Him our praise, (2) give Him our thanks, and (3) give Him our whole heart—freely sharing everything that's inside. But we *shouldn't* (1) go through the motions of an empty ritual, (2) approach Him with wrong motives, (3) use our devotional times as a means of getting something, (4) treat these special moments as optional in our lives. God wants us to spend time with Him. It pleases Him, and it plugs our lives into the ultimate Power Source. And if we stay plugged in, those high-voltage spiritual zaps will gradually transform us into high-voltage Christians!

TALK TO GOD

As you pray, encourage your child to (1) thank Jesus for being our source for good things in life and (2) ask the Lord to help us stay spiritually healthy through prayer and Bible reading.

24

MY SUFFICIENCY

And God is able to bless you abundantly, so that in all things at all times,
having all that you need, you will abound in every good work.

2 Corinthians 9:8

FAMILY QUEST

Ahead of time, familiarize yourself with Exodus 16:1–36. God had just delivered the Israelites from bondage in Egypt, parting the Red Sea and giving them miracle after miracle as Moses led them to the Promised Land. But now the Israelites are starting to complain, especially about the lack of food and water. In this passage, God comes through again—this time with quail and manna. Retell a kid-friendly version of this story. Emphasize the message that God is our sufficiency—He provides all we need.

TALK IT OUT

- Can you think of a time God gave our family exactly what we needed—right when we needed it?
- Read Matthew 6:25–27. Why does God tell us not to worry?
- How does it make you feel to know that God provides all we need?

PARENT-CHILD CONNECTION

Help your child understand that (1) life has its ups and downs—often moving from peace to challenge, and usually back to peace again—and (2) God will take care of us through every season. He will protect us during the storms and will celebrate with us each time the sun returns. He cries when we cry, and He takes pleasure in our happiness. He feels what we feel and walks with us every step. Why? Because He is our Creator, our Father, our Friend. . .and especially our Sufficiency. God knows what we need exactly when we need it. He will never abandon us, nor will He leave us alone when life is painful. Jesus is the God of all comfort, the God whose name is "The One Who Will Be There with You."

TALK TO GOD

As you pray, encourage your child to (1) thank Jesus for meeting our needs and (2) ask the Lord to help us not to worry.

25
MY TEACHER

When he had finished washing their feet, he put on his clothes and returned to his place. "Do you understand what I have done for you?" he asked them. "You call me 'Teacher' and 'Lord,' and rightly so, for that is what I am. Now that I, your Lord and Teacher, have washed your feet, you also should wash one another's feet. I have set you an example that you should do as I have done for you."

JOHN 13:12–15

FAMILY QUEST

Pull out a washbasin, soap, and towels and follow Christ's example: scrub each other's feet. As you do this, talk about the example our Lord and Teacher set for us.

TALK IT OUT

- What lesson was Jesus teaching us?
- Think about the teachers you know. What makes them so good at what they do?
- Jesus teaches us many things. Can you think of five things He wants us to learn?

PARENT-CHILD CONNECTION

After washing His disciples' feet, Jesus said, "Now that I, your Lord and Teacher, have washed your feet, you also should wash one another's feet. I have set you an example that you should do as I have done for you" (John 13:14–15). Throughout the New Testament, Jesus often teaches us to "go and do likewise"; to never keep His lessons to ourselves, but to imitate them; to follow His example and share them with others. And today's lesson gives us a perfect demonstration of what God considers to be real greatness. It's not found in world leaders, professional athletes, or

Hollywood superstars. It's not even found in the great spiritual leaders of our time. These aren't the ones whom God considers to be great. Instead, according to the Lord, "whoever wants to become great among you must be your servant, and whoever wants to be first must be your slave—just as the Son of Man did not come to be served, but to serve" (Matthew 20:26–28). This is the key to greatness. This is what our Teacher wants us to live out in our walk and our witness. Encourage your children to take to heart the Teacher's lessons. . .and go and do likewise.

TALK TO GOD

As you pray, encourage your child to (1) thank Jesus for being the ultimate Teacher and (2) ask the Lord to help him "go and do" what Jesus teaches in the Bible.

Part Two

My Trust in God

He Is. . .

26
ALL-KNOWING

You know when I sit and when I rise;
you perceive my thoughts from afar.
PSALM 139:2

FAMILY QUEST

Have everyone pick something to think about but don't tell what it is! Then, have Mom or Dad try to guess the others' thoughts. Can they? Then read the verse and talk it out.

TALK IT OUT

- Why didn't Mom/Dad know what you were thinking?
- Now consider this: God knows all your thoughts. He knows exactly what you need, and He loves you more than you can imagine. How does this make you feel?
- Since God is all-knowing, it is okay to be completely honest with Him about our hurts, doubts, and fears. What might you have a hard time being completely honest with God about?

PARENT-CHILD CONNECTION

Sometimes it can be overwhelming to think that God knows all of our thoughts. Reassure your child that it is a good thing that God is all-knowing. He knows our hearts and our good intentions. He isn't trying to catch us messing up. He speaks to us through our minds and emotions. Our confessions to Him do more for us than for Him. He already knows what we do and think. But opening up and telling God everything is freeing. It is through that act of confession that He speaks to us. We grow during these times of honesty.

TALK TO GOD

As you pray, encourage your child to (1) thank Jesus for knowing us inside and out and (2) ask the Lord to remind us how much He loves us.

27

ALL-POWERFUL

I pray that. . .you may know. . .his incomparably great power for us who believe. That power is the same as the mighty strength he exerted when he raised Christ from the dead.
EPHESIANS 1:18–20

FAMILY QUEST

Pull out paper, markers, and crayons and have your child engage in a creative assignment: "Draw something powerful or list some things you think of as powerful."

TALK IT OUT

- What did you think of as powerful?
- Do you know anything powerful enough to raise someone from the dead?
- God is all-powerful. He raised Jesus from the dead, and He wants you to have His power in your life. What would you want God to help you with today?

PARENT-CHILD CONNECTION

This conversation will probably include a question from your child that sounds like this: "If God is all-powerful, why can't He heal everyone and make all of the bad stuff go away?" This is a good opportunity to discuss the reality of living in a broken world. This world is not perfect, and things will never be the way we wish they were. But God wants to help us through it. He cares for us and uses His power to offer us an eternity with Him. He overcame death for us. Now that's a good use of power!

TALK TO GOD

As you pray, encourage your child to (1) thank Jesus for being all-powerful and (2) ask God to show His power in some specific way.

28
ALL-SUFFICIENT

His divine power has given us everything we need for a godly life through our knowledge of him who called us by his own glory and goodness.
2 PETER 1:3

FAMILY QUEST

Grab a puzzle off the shelf and have everyone work on it together. Once it's complete, take out a few of the pieces and see if it still looks like the same picture.

TALK IT OUT

- Did the picture look the same without all the pieces?
- Discuss the "big picture" of life. Who holds all the pieces to the puzzle of our lives?
- How can you receive all the pieces from God?

PARENT-CHILD CONNECTION

This topic connects well with the other devotions that discuss the characteristics of God. He is all we need. And He uses all of His abilities and traits to help us know Him better. His power, love, and mercy (not to mention all of the others) come together for our benefit. This amazing diversity makes Him all-sufficient.

TALK TO GOD

As you pray, encourage your child to (1) thank Jesus for providing all the pieces for his future and (2) ask the Lord to help him have a heart open to God's direction.

29
ALL-WISE

*Oh, the depth of the riches of
the wisdom and knowledge of God!*
ROMANS 11:33

FAMILY QUEST

Before today's lesson, gather information about King Solomon. Take a few minutes to tell his story: how he got so smart, as well as what he accomplished in life. Next, engage your child in an amazing truth: God is all-wise!

TALK IT OUT

- The Bible tells us that God knows all things. This means He is even wiser than Solomon. God is all-wise. Being wise includes being smart, but it also includes knowing what's right and doing it. Share about a time when you knew what was right and did it.
- Where does real wisdom come from?
- How does God make us wise?

PARENT-CHILD CONNECTION

Kids are very familiar with the concept of "right and wrong." And they usually have a good grasp on the concept of consequences for their actions. But "wisdom" is a little tricky. It is a more abstract idea that some younger kids may struggle to understand. Tell your kids a story from your own life or a story about a friend to help them see that wisdom is needed in everyday life. A few good examples may help them to see the difference between being smart and being wise.

TALK TO GOD

As you pray, encourage your child to (1) thank Jesus for being so wise and (2) ask Him to help us to be wise.

30
ALMIGHTY

*Whoever dwells in the shelter of the
Most High will rest in the shadow of the Almighty.*
PSALM 91:1

FAMILY QUEST

Play a game of hide-and-seek.

TALK IT OUT

- Where would you go if you were scared and needed a safe place to hide?
- How can you find "shelter" in "the shadow of the Almighty"? How can He be your hiding place?
- How is God our Father *almighty*? How does this image make you feel?

PARENT-CHILD CONNECTION

Again, this is a great opportunity for you to share a personal story from your life. Let your kids know of a time when you were scared or lonely and God helped you. It is important to let them know that things don't always work out the way we think they should. His ways are always good, but often different from our expectations.

TALK TO GOD

As you pray, encourage your child to (1) thank Jesus for His love and strength and (2) ask the Lord to help her run to Him for safety and protection.

31

ALPHA AND OMEGA

*"I am the Alpha and the Omega,
the First and the Last, the Beginning and the End."*
REVELATION 22:13

FAMILY QUEST

Head into the kitchen for some family time. Roll out some cookie dough and have your child shape it into the symbols for alpha and omega. If you don't know what these symbols look like, stop and do a little research together to find out.

TALK IT OUT

- What are "alpha" and "omega"?
- What does Jesus mean when He says He is the "Alpha and Omega"?
- Is anyone else "alpha" and/or "omega"?
- What does this tell us about Jesus' ability to provide for us?

PARENT-CHILD CONNECTION

Today's topic may seem like a rather large concept to discuss with your children. But seeing God as the Alpha and Omega speaks to His true identity and will help them begin to form a better understanding of who He is. It's okay if you can't fully explain this description to them. Some things are too big for any of us to totally understand. It's fine to let your kids know that a little mystery is okay. Our lack of understanding doesn't take anything away from God's character. It helps us to grasp the reality that He is bigger and more brilliant than we could ever understand.

TALK TO GOD

As you pray, encourage your child to (1) thank Jesus for all the things He provides for us and (2) ask the Lord to help her to trust Jesus to provide everything needed.

32

BENEVOLENT

And my God will meet all your needs
according to the riches of his glory in Christ Jesus.
PHILIPPIANS 4:19

FAMILY QUEST

Ask your children to write a definition of the word *benevolent* and some words that are similar. Now look it up to find the actual meaning. Once you have discussed what the word means, plan with your children to undertake an act of benevolence.

TALK IT OUT

- How close did you come to knowing what *benevolent* means?
- Think about the stories you've heard about Jesus. Which one best shows Him as benevolent? Why?
- What can you do if you are afraid that your needs won't be met?

PARENT-CHILD CONNECTION

Giving a tithe to your local church is a good example of how God provides for us. He supplies us with all we need and only asks for 10 percent back. With this 10 percent He provides for the mission of your church as it ministers to many people throughout the week. We are an important part of God's plan and mission. By trusting Him to provide for us, we are free to help others and support the overall mission.

TALK TO GOD

As you pray, encourage your child to (1) thank Jesus for providing for his needs as well as the family's needs, and (2) ask the Lord to help everyone in the family to respond in a benevolent way to the needs around them.

33
COMPASSIONATE

Jesus had compassion on them and touched their eyes.
Immediately they received their sight and followed him.
MATTHEW 20:34

FAMILY QUEST

As a family, make a list of people you know who have great needs in their lives (health, family, finances, etc.). On that same list, jot down how you can show them compassion.

TALK IT OUT

- Does God know all the needs of everyone in the world?
- Does He have compassion for those who are not healed?
- What is *compassion*?
- As a Christian, how can you show compassion to people around you?

PARENT-CHILD CONNECTION

A good way to explain compassion to your kids is to show them that it is "love in action." Compassion begins in our hearts and is then shown through our actions. God has shown us this kind of love, and now it is our turn to show this kind of love to others.

TALK TO GOD

As you pray, encourage your child to (1) thank Jesus for His compassion and (2) ask the Lord to show her how to be compassionate to others.

34
CONSISTENT

Jesus Christ is the same yesterday and today and forever.
HEBREWS 13:8

FAMILY QUEST

Help your children understand what the word *consistent* means. Make a list of the things you do every day in the same way. Make another list of all the things in your life that constantly change.

TALK IT OUT

- How does it make you feel when things change?
- How does knowing that Jesus does not change make you feel?
- In what way can we be *consistent* just like Jesus? (Praying regularly, reading God's Word, showing love to others.)

PARENT-CHILD CONNECTION

Some younger kids may have a hard time distinguishing between being consistent and never changing. God's character never changes. He always loves us and is working to bring us closer to Him. But the ways in which He does this may change from situation to situation. It is important to help kids understand this so they don't become frustrated later in life because God is not interacting with them like He has in the past.

TALK TO GOD

As you pray, encourage your child to (1) thank Jesus that He never changes and (2) ask the Lord to help him feel His presence especially when he must face change.

35
COURAGEOUS

*But Christ is faithful as the Son over God's house.
And we are his house, if indeed we hold firmly
to our confidence and the hope in which we glory.*
HEBREWS 3:6

FAMILY QUEST

Before you meet, pull out three large bowls and fill each one with three different items: place cooked spaghetti in one bowl, Jell-O in another, and gummy worm candies in the third. Next, place the bowls in brown paper sacks. Dare your kids to come forward, put on a blindfold, and—without seeing what's inside—bravely stick one hand in each bag and feel the items. To add to the drama make up a story: Tell everyone that you just returned from the meat department at the supermarket and asked the butcher to let you take home some "spare parts." Say something like this: "Who has the courage to relinquish their hand to my mystery bags?" Have them describe the experience and try to guess what's inside. And then turn the conversation to the subject of *courage*.

TALK IT OUT

- What went through your mind as you touched each item?
- Did you have to muster up courage? Why or why not?
- Describe those moments in your life when you need extra courage.
- Think about how brave Jesus was during His ministry on earth—especially when He went to the cross for us. How does that make you feel? Do you trust that He will give you courage when you need it? (Explain your answer.)

PARENT-CHILD CONNECTION

Open your Bible and read 2 Corinthians 12:1–10. Talk about Paul's "thorn" and about how Jesus gave this follower the grace and the strength to cope with his adversity. Tell your child this: "When bad things happen in our lives—when we feel pain, problems, and pressure—God has not abandoned us. We can turn our problems over to Jesus. We can ask Him for the strength and courage to face tomorrow."

TALK TO GOD

As you pray, encourage your child to (1) thank Jesus for His courage and (2) ask the Lord for help in being braver—especially when life feels scary.

36
DECISIVE

*As the time approached for him to be taken up
to heaven, Jesus resolutely set out for Jerusalem.*
LUKE 9:51

FAMILY QUEST

Jesus was a man on a mission. Time after time, He knew what He had to do, and He did it decisively. Encourage your kids to follow His example. Pull out some notepads and ask them to list various decisions that they must make now, especially the ones that can end up affecting their future. In other words, deciding whether or not to do their homework, brush their teeth, eat good food that fuels their bodies. . .commit to following Jesus.

TALK IT OUT

- Why did Jesus set out for Jerusalem?
- What do you think are the most important decisions in life?
- Sometimes we have to make difficult decisions. How can Jesus' example help you be decisive about unpleasant decisions?

PARENT-CHILD CONNECTION

This is a good reminder that God is always working for our good. He is using His amazing abilities to care for us. He knows that our lives will be better if we stay close to Him, and He has given us so many ways to do this. Praying, reading our Bible, being a part of a church, and so many other practices help us to stay connected. He has given us these things so we can stay strong and be ready when difficult decisions come our way.

TALK TO GOD

As you pray, encourage your child to (1) ask Jesus to help her make decisions that are pleasing to God and (2) thank Him for providing comfort and encouragement when hard decisions have to be made.

37
ETERNAL

"I am the Alpha and the Omega," says the Lord God,
"who is, and who was, and who is to come, the Almighty."
REVELATION 1:8

FAMILY QUEST

Have your child draw a big circle with no beginning or ending point. Parents may also use their rings as an example. Discuss the meaning of *eternal*.

TALK IT OUT

- Where is the beginning and the ending?
- Are we eternal? How is God different from us?
- Does God's love for us ever end?

PARENT-CHILD CONNECTION

This is a difficult topic for most adults to grasp. But it is important to begin this discussion when your kids are young. They need to know that God is eternal even if they can't fully understand it. God isn't just the good guy who can be replaced by another good guy down the line. He is God—always and forever!

TALK TO GOD

As you pray, encourage your child to (1) thank Jesus for always loving him and (2) ask the Lord to help him walk with Him and choose to love Him.

38
EVERYWHERE

Where can I go from your Spirit? Where can I
flee from your presence? If I go up to the heavens,
you are there; if I make my bed in the depths, you are there.
PSALM 139:7–8

FAMILY QUEST

Take a globe or a map of the world and locate as closely as possible the place where you live. Locate three places that are as far as possible from where you live. Use the Internet or an atlas to find how many people live in each of these places, what the climate is like, and how near it is to an ocean or mountains.

TALK IT OUT

- How far would we have to go to get away from God?
- How is God present in these far-off places?
- How does this make us feel when we go to school or camp or on vacation?

PARENT-CHILD CONNECTION

God's omnipresence should be a comforting reality for your child as long as they know that God's love and compassion also follow us everywhere. If kids see God as their protector, then His omnipresence is a good thing. But if they fear God, then this can be a scary reality. Let your child know that it is a good thing for God to be "everywhere." He is always available when we need Him.

TALK TO GOD

As you pray, encourage your child to (1) thank God for being everywhere and (2) ask the Lord to open her eyes to see Him in whatever new places she might go.

39

FAITHFUL

God is faithful, who has called you into
fellowship with his Son, Jesus Christ our Lord.
1 CORINTHIANS 1:9

FAMILY QUEST

Things change: the weather, our moods—even what's for dinner. But God stays the same. Pull out a notepad and list ten (or more) things around you that might change, as well as ten (or more) things about God that *never* change.

TALK IT OUT

- Who is always faithful to you?
- Are you faithful to your friends and family? God?
- Is it easier for you or God to be faithful? How is the Lord faithful?

PARENT-CHILD CONNECTION

Loyalty is an important character trait. Being faithful to your commitments will have a significant impact on your life. Just like God is faithful to us, He wants us to be faithful to Him and to others. We were created to be in proper relationship with both God and other people. Encourage your kids to follow Christ's example by being faithful.

TALK TO GOD

As you pray, encourage your child to (1) thank Jesus for being faithful and unchanging and (2) ask the Lord to help him be a faithful friend to others.

40

FORGIVING

If we confess our sins, he is faithful and just and will
forgive us our sins and purify us from all unrighteousness.
1 JOHN 1:9

FAMILY QUEST

The cross is an unforgettable reminder of Jesus Christ and what He has done for those who have given their hearts to Him: He paid the penalty for our sins, He has completely forgiven us, and He invites us to live forever with Him! Celebrate together by making some cross necklaces. Be creative: use pieces of sticks and leather, pipe cleaners, or beads and string.

TALK IT OUT

- The word *confess* means "to agree with." We need to agree with God that what we have done is wrong. Do you find this easy or hard to do? Why?
- Why is it important to "agree with God" whenever we sin?
- If we admit that what we've done is wrong and ask God to forgive us, does He really forget the wrong things we've done? Read Psalm 103:12.

PARENT-CHILD CONNECTION

Kids are usually afraid to admit when they have done something wrong. They learn early that there are consequences for their actions. So *confession* does not sound like something they will be willing to do. Yes, there are consequences. But it is extremely important that we discuss our failures with God. He is the One who offers forgiveness and can bring restoration to us. Please encourage your kids not to avoid having these tough conversations with Christ.

TALK TO GOD

As you pray, encourage your child to (1) thank Jesus for dying on the cross and giving us eternal life with Him and (2) tell the Lord that she is sorry for messing up at times.

41

GENTLE

*"Take my yoke upon you and learn from me, for I am gentle
and humble in heart, and you will find rest for your souls."*
MATTHEW 11:29

FAMILY QUEST

Close your eyes and have your child describe God. Encourage him to explain God's looks, His voice, His face, His actions, etc. Now have your child describe what it would be like to meet God.

TALK IT OUT

- How would you describe God?
- Do you ever picture Him as gentle?
- When is God powerful? When is He gentle?

PARENT-CHILD CONNECTION

As you use this devotional guide with your child, you will be talking a lot about the character of God. Be careful in your conversations that your child doesn't become scared of God. We should be very respectful of Him, but He does not want us to be fearful. Understanding that God is gentle is significant as your child develops his own image of God.

TALK TO GOD

As you pray, encourage your child to (1) thank Jesus for loving us and (2) ask the Lord for help and peace in times of turmoil.

42

GOOD

God saw all that he had made, and it was very good.
And there was evening, and there was morning—the sixth day.
GENESIS 1:31

FAMILY QUEST

God stepped back and looked at everything He had created, and He was happy. He is the source of all that is good. And we were created out of that goodness. Amazing! As a family, make some creations of your own: cool clay people and animals, Lego towers, or artwork using markers and finger paint. Take turns sharing the good points about your creations.

TALK IT OUT

- What does it mean to be *good*?
- What are some good things in your life?
- Who is the source of these good things? Who is the ultimate source?

PARENT-CHILD CONNECTION

God is the source of all goodness in the world. He was very happy when He created this world and all of the people in it. And His goodness continues to shine through His amazing creation and His people. Without this source to tap into, we would not even know how to be good. We are reminded daily of His love as we recognize His work in the good deeds of His people. Help your kids to "see" God's goodness in the small, everyday events in life.

TALK TO GOD

As you pray, encourage your child to (1) thank Jesus for His goodness and (2) express to the Lord how happy she is for a family to grow up in.

43

GRACIOUS

But God demonstrates his own love for us in this:
While we were still sinners, Christ died for us.
ROMANS 5:8

FAMILY QUEST

Take turns sharing the last good thing you did for someone else.

TALK IT OUT

- Why did you do something good for someone else?
- How did they respond? How did it make you feel?
- What did Jesus do for you? What has He done for you today?

PARENT-CHILD CONNECTION

Being thankful for the blessings in our lives should prompt us to share with others. This response doesn't always come naturally and needs to be taught to kids at an early age. Sharing within the family sets a good example for how we should pass our blessings on to those outside of our homes. Sharing is an excellent way to say thank you.

TALK TO GOD

As you pray, encourage your child to (1) thank Jesus for coming to earth to show us grace by bringing us salvation, and (2) ask the Lord for help to be more like Him by doing good for others, even without being asked.

44
HOLY

But just as he who called you is holy, so be holy in all you do;
for it is written: "Be holy, because I am holy."
1 PETER 1:15–16

FAMILY QUEST

Have each family member do a household search for a useful item. Talk about the purpose of each object. Explain that *holy* means "to be set apart for God's use."

TALK IT OUT

- Flip through the four Gospels and find examples of Christ's holy behavior. How did Jesus demonstrate holiness to others? How should we live it out?
- Read 1 Peter 1:15–16. As a family, how can we help each other live holy lives?
- How does God feel about us when we don't act very holy?

PARENT-CHILD CONNECTION

People have a lot of opinions about what it means to be holy. But the passage above simplifies it for us. We are to be holy as Jesus is holy. This means we should be Christlike. That is what the word *Christian* means. So as we study the characteristics of God and the life and ministry of Jesus Christ, we learn how we, too, are supposed to live. A life of love, compassion, wisdom, obedience, sacrifice, and joy would resemble God. When we learn about God, we are also learning how to live our own lives.

TALK TO GOD

As you pray, encourage your child to (1) thank Jesus for setting the perfect example for holiness and (2) ask the Lord to build in him the courage to follow Christ's example.

45

IMMORTAL

God, the blessed and only Ruler, the King of kings and Lord of lords,
who alone is immortal and who lives in unapproachable light,
whom no one has seen or can see. To him be honor and might forever. Amen.
1 TIMOTHY 6:15–16

FAMILY QUEST

Ask your child what happens all around her in nature in the spring. How does nature change in the summer? What about autumn? How do the trees and flowers change in winter? Now focus your talk on a nearby evergreen. How does it change? Explain that evergreens are not immortal and do change somewhat, but because they are always green, they give us an idea of what *immortal* means: unchanging, lasting.

TALK IT OUT

- Jesus is immortal—that means He'll never die. Can you think of anything that will never die?
- Why is it important that Jesus is immortal?
- Will we be immortal like Jesus when we get to heaven? Explain.

PARENT-CHILD CONNECTION

Immortality is a common theme in movies and television shows. It seems that every superhero is immortal as long as they stay away from their one weakness. Kids will tend to think of God in this way. But He is way more than that. He is the only real immortal being. Help your kids to understand that there is a difference between our very real God and fictional characters.

TALK TO GOD

As you pray, encourage your child to (1) thank Jesus that He will live forever and (2) ask the Lord to help her never forget that God created her to live forever in heaven with God.

46

IN CONTROL

*And God placed all things under his feet and appointed him
to be head over everything for the church, which is his body,
the fullness of him who fills everything in every way.*

EPHESIANS 1:22–23

FAMILY QUEST

Life can get crazy. People and circumstances can be scary, but we can be confident that God is in control! To help you remember this, make a Bible bookmark. Pull out your construction paper, scissors, markers, glitter, and glue. Write the following on your bookmark: "I trust the Bible: Jesus Christ rules!" (Ephesians 1:22).

TALK IT OUT

- What kinds of things scare you?
- The Bible says God has "placed all things under [Jesus'] feet." That means He is in charge of everything. How does it make you feel knowing that He is in control?
- What does this tell us about Jesus' ability to take care of us?

PARENT-CHILD CONNECTION

Encourage your kids to explore the Bible on their own. Let them pick any passage and then discuss it with them. This may lead to some very interesting conversations as you talk about some of the challenges that people faced in the Bible. This exercise will help kids see that everyone throughout time has had to deal with some difficult situations. God helped them just like He will help us. The Bible offers us an amazing history of God's faithfulness to His people.

TALK TO GOD

As you pray, encourage your child to (1) thank Jesus for His authority and (2) ask the Lord for more faith, especially when life feels scary.

47

INFINITE

Great is our Lord and mighty in power;
his understanding has no limit.
PSALM 147:5

FAMILY QUEST

Have your children quiz you on your favorite subject. Allow them to ask questions until you run out of answers. Now discuss God and His never-ending knowledge.

TALK IT OUT

- Does God really know everything?
- What about stuff that hasn't happened yet?
- How does it make you feel to realize He knows everything about you?

PARENT-CHILD CONNECTION

Isn't it amazing that we have a personal connection with God, who knows everything? His understanding is not limited to the past or to what we want Him to know. He knows everything. As we seek Him and His ways, He will continue to help us grow in wisdom as well.

TALK TO GOD

As you pray, encourage your child to (1) thank Jesus for His love and understanding and (2) ask the Lord to help her respect His wisdom.

48

A JEALOUS GOD

"You shall not make for yourself an image in the form of anything in heaven above or on the earth beneath or in the waters below. You shall not bow down to them or worship them; for I, the LORD your God, am a jealous God, punishing the children for the sin of the parents to the third and fourth generation of those who hate me, but showing love to a thousand generations of those who love me and keep my commandments."

EXODUS 20:4–6

FAMILY QUEST

Before today's lesson, familiarize yourself with Exodus 32:1–24. In your own words—and in a way that's appropriate for your child's age—share this story. Be creative and use props: puppets, stuffed animals, and sound effects.

TALK IT OUT

- What did these people do that made God so angry?
- What does the word *jealous* mean?
- Why do you think God is jealous when it comes to our hearts and what we worship?

PARENT-CHILD CONNECTION

Jealousy is often seen as a bad thing. Kids are correctly taught not to be jealous or envious. But God's jealousy for us is different. He loves us so much and wants us to love Him, too. He continues to pursue us even when we want nothing to do with Him. And His heart is broken every time we walk away and embrace something else. Let your children know that His love continues to reach out to us regardless of our actions. It is when we worship Him only that we make Him happy.

TALK TO GOD

As you pray, encourage your child to (1) thank Jesus for setting us right when we go wrong and (2) ask the Lord to help us put Him first.

49

JUST

*"Listen to me, my people; hear me, my nation: Instruction will
go out from me; my justice will become a light to the nations."*
ISAIAH 51:4

FAMILY QUEST

Have everyone make a list of words that describe the words *just* and
justice. Now go back and circle each word that applies to God's justice.

TALK IT OUT

- How is God "just"?
- Is God's justice different from the way humans are "just"?
- How is His justice a light to the nations?

PARENT-CHILD CONNECTION

Just is not a word that most kids are familiar with. It's important
for kids to understand that there is a difference between human justice
and God's justice. His ways are pure and just. Human ways are often
complicated by personal agendas and frustration. Help your children to
know that even though we can be let down by humans, God will never
let us down.

TALK TO GOD

As you pray, encourage your child to (1) thank Jesus that He is a just
God and (2) ask the Lord to help him be just.

50
LIVING

He told them, "This is what is written:
The Messiah will suffer and rise from the dead on the third day."
LUKE 24:46

FAMILY QUEST

It's amazing that God would come to earth as Jesus. But it's even more amazing that He died on the cross and then rose from the grave. He even walked around and visited with His friends after His resurrection. And He is alive now. As a reminder, plant some seeds in plastic cups. Place the cups in a warm place like the top of your refrigerator. Once they begin to sprout, place them on the windowsill of a sunny window. Water as needed.

TALK IT OUT

- Do you know the story of Jesus?
- Why do we celebrate Jesus' resurrection? Which holiday is that?
- Why is this important to you?

PARENT-CHILD CONNECTION

Easter is often seen as the holiday that celebrates the coming of spring and warm weather. The Easter bunny, egg hunts, and chocolate are all fun for kids. But it is vital that they know the real reason we celebrate Easter. Jesus' resurrection is a fundamental event for the world. It is our path to salvation. This calls for a much bigger celebration than a day of candy and games.

TALK TO GOD

As you pray, encourage your child to (1) thank Jesus for being willing to die on the cross and (2) praise the Lord for His power to save us.

51

LONG-SUFFERING

*But concerning Israel he says, "All day long I have
held out my hands to a disobedient and obstinate people."*

ROMANS 10:21

FAMILY QUEST

Ask your child to draw a picture of God longing for His people.
Have her show how He waits for them as they make both good and bad
decisions.

TALK IT OUT

- How long will God wait on you to obey Him?
- Do you make Him happy or sad?
- Is He quick to forgive you? How does it make Him feel when
  you seek Him?

PARENT-CHILD CONNECTION

Patience is a hard trait to possess regardless of age. Most of the
examples you come up with while discussing patience with your child
may be about the times when you were impatient. And since children
haven't had all of the practice of adults, being patient is even harder
for them. That is what makes God's patience so much more amazing.
He continues to love and pursue us throughout our lives. This is a great
opportunity for you to teach your child to be thankful for God's long-
suffering.

TALK TO GOD

As you pray, encourage your child to (1) thank Jesus for His patience
and (2) ask the Lord to help her obey Him.

52
LOVE

Dear friends, let us love one another, for love comes from God.
Everyone who loves has been born of God and knows God.
1 JOHN 4:7

FAMILY QUEST

We use the word *love* almost every day. There are so many types of love and ways to love each other. It's amazing that they all come from the same source: God. Bake a giant cookie in the shape of a heart. Decorate it together, and then enjoy a sweet feast!

TALK IT OUT

- Whom do you love? Who loves you?
- What are the different kinds of love?
- How has God shown His love for you? How can you show love to others?

PARENT-CHILD CONNECTION

Love is a common theme in songs and books, and it's easy for kids to lump them all together into one category. But there are so many different kinds of love. Romantic love is different than the love you have for your country. The love that a parent has for his child is different than the love he has for his favorite football team. But God's love supersedes all of those. And it is the source of all of the other kinds of love. This is a topic that can easily be carried on in the future. Point it out when you hear a song on the radio or watch a kids' television show. It will really help your child see the difference.

TALK TO GOD

As you pray, encourage your child to (1) thank Jesus for being the source of all true love and (2) ask the Lord for help as he reaches out to others.

53
MAJESTIC

*For I have always been mindful of your unfailing
love and have lived in reliance on your faithfulness.*
PSALM 26:3

FAMILY QUEST

Grab some construction paper, scissors, markers, glue, and glitter. Have each person cut their paper into the shape of a star. It can be one big star or a couple of smaller ones. Decorate the stars with markers and glitter. Take some time to imagine what it must be like to be in outer space. Talk about the stars, sun, and planets. Discuss how awesome it is that God made all of it. How He knows all of the stars, animals, and people in our world. He is truly majestic!

TALK IT OUT

- How big is God?
- Do you think He enjoys all of the wonderful things He created? Does He enjoy you?
- In what ways is God majestic?

PARENT-CHILD CONNECTION

It's amazing to think about how majestic God is. But it's even more amazing to think that He knows and cares about each and every one of us. That's right. The God of the universe chooses to be in relationship with us. It's hard to believe when we stop and think about His majesty. Loving and caring for each individual is one way that God shows how big He is. No one else even comes close to being capable of such love.

TALK TO GOD

As you pray, encourage your child to (1) thank God for creating us and (2) ask the Lord to help her always remember how majestic He is.

54
MERCIFUL

*The Lord our God is
merciful and forgiving.*
DANIEL 9:9

FAMILY QUEST

Grab a dictionary and look up the word *merciful*. Talk about how we need God's mercy in our lives because we aren't perfect. His love for us is so great that He keeps giving us chance after chance. He knows our hearts and knows when we are really trying to love Him.

TALK IT OUT
- What does the word *compassion* mean?
- Why does God love us so much?
- How can we help others enjoy God's amazing love?

PARENT-CHILD CONNECTION

"Have mercy" is an old saying that is usually reserved for little old ladies. Your kids may never have even heard this expression. But it is a reminder that we have to intentionally extend mercy to others. For God, however, compassion is in His very nature. And when we show this same type of love and mercy to others, it is a small representation of how God loves us. Kids live in a world where they learn early to protect themselves and their belongings. It's not going to come naturally to them to extend mercy to someone who may have done them wrong. But it's a good time to begin teaching them this valuable character trait.

TALK TO GOD

As you pray, encourage your child to (1) thank Jesus for His abounding love and (2) ask the Lord to help him show more compassion to others.

55

MORAL

But the wisdom that comes from heaven is first of all pure; then peace-loving, considerate, submissive, full of mercy and good fruit, impartial and sincere.
JAMES 3:17

FAMILY QUEST

Play a game of truth or dare. Make sure all of your dares are safe and fun. Give extra attention to your truth questions. Fashion them as questions that present a moral dilemma, such as, "If your friend stole something from the store, would you tell on them?"

TALK IT OUT

- Is it easy or hard to do the right thing?
- How do you feel when you make a bad decision? And when you make a good one?
- In what ways is God our example of how to be moral?

PARENT-CHILD CONNECTION

Playing truth or dare with your kids can be a little dangerous. Chances are, they will ask you some difficult questions as well. This is an opportunity to be open and honest with them. You may learn more about your child by her questions than by the ones you are asking. Once again, this is the type of game that can be picked up later as you continue to teach your child through conversation.

TALK TO GOD

As you pray, encourage your child to (1) thank the Lord for being our moral guide and (2) ask God to help her make good decisions every day.

56

MOST HIGH

"However, the Most High does not live in houses made by human hands. As the prophet says: 'Heaven is my throne, and the earth is my footstool. What kind of house will you build for me? says the Lord. Or where will my resting place be? Has not my hand made all these things?' "

ACTS 7:48–50

FAMILY QUEST

Draw a picture of what you think heaven looks like. Now discuss how you think it will *feel* to be there.

TALK IT OUT
- Where is heaven? (Why can God see us, but we can't see Him?)
- How can we go to heaven?
- Who else is in heaven?

PARENT-CHILD CONNECTION

From an early age, most people have formed an idea of what heaven is like. Most of our images come from movies and books. And for those who attend Sunday school, there are some correct images as well. But all we know of heaven is what we can learn from the Bible. It is our source for what to expect. Help your kids to marvel at the unknown aspects of heaven. We don't know the specifics of how it will all work. But we do know that we get to be in the presence of God for eternity. And that will be more amazing than anything we could ever dream up.

TALK TO GOD

As you pray, encourage your child to (1) thank Jesus for making a place like heaven and (2) ask the Lord for help to think more often about Him throughout the day.

57

NEAR

Yet you are near, LORD,
and all your commands are true.
PSALM 119:151

FAMILY QUEST

Play a game of hide-and-seek. Now ask your child if he can hide from God. Talk about how God is always near, no matter where we are or what we are doing.

TALK IT OUT

- How can God be near every one of His children at once?
- Do you ever feel God? (Is He still there when you can't feel Him?)
- Does God see you when you are making a bad decision?

PARENT-CHILD CONNECTION

Reassure your child that having God always near is a good thing. He is not there to spy on us or to catch us messing up. He is there because He likes being with us. He cares for us and wants to help us as we live our everyday lives. This desire is why He continues to forgive and love us on both the good days and the bad days.

TALK TO GOD

As you pray, encourage your child to (1) thank Jesus for His nearness and (2) ask the Lord to help him make good decisions.

58

THE ONE TRUE VOICE

The voice of the LORD is powerful;
the voice of the LORD is majestic.
PSALM 29:4

FAMILY QUEST

Take turns demonstrating different types of voices: everything you can think of from a loud and powerful voice to a soft and gentle one. Discuss how it makes you feel when you hear each voice.

TALK IT OUT

- What do you think God's voice sounds like? Do you think His voice sounds like the ones you came up with?
- What are some of the ways God talks to His children? What is the main way God talks to us today?
- What can you do to hear God better?

PARENT-CHILD CONNECTION

Refer to some of God's other attributes that you have learned about in this devotional guide. How do they connect with the "voice of God"? God speaks to us through His Word, prayer, preachers, authors, and that small feeling we get in our gut when we are faced with a difficult decision. We will always benefit when we listen to what God is telling us. He always works in our favor.

TALK TO GOD

As you pray, encourage your child to (1) thank Jesus for having the one true voice we can trust and (2) ask the Lord for help in hearing Him more clearly.

59

PATIENT

For the LORD is good and his love endures forever;
his faithfulness continues through all generations.
PSALM 100:5

FAMILY QUEST

Play a game of Simon Says. As the parent, give commands that are simple and fun. But give a lot of commands without saying "Simon Says," too. Make them wait for a command where they can move around.

TALK IT OUT

- Was it hard to wait for a command where you could move around?
- Do you like to wait? Why or why not?
- In what ways does God wait for us?
- Do you think God likes to wait?

PARENT-CHILD CONNECTION

No one likes to be without power. Even in a simple game of Simon Says, your kids will probably want to have their turn at giving the commands. Even though God has all the power in the universe, He waits for us. He always has throughout time. He even helped Adam and Eve after they sinned. And He continues to wait for us today. Help your kids appreciate God's faithfulness.

TALK TO GOD

As you pray, encourage your child to (1) thank Jesus for His abounding love and (2) ask the Lord to help him show more patience toward others.

60

PERSISTENT

*"I am the Living One; I was dead,
and now look, I am alive for ever and ever!"*
REVELATION 1:18

FAMILY QUEST

Talk about things around you that never seem to go away—it might be a mountain, the sky, or the human race. Think about how God lived before all of these things, and He will live after they are all gone. And the whole time He is reaching out to us.

TALK IT OUT

- What does *persistent* mean? Have you ever tried to do something forever?
- Why does God stay with us?
- How does His persistence make you feel?

PARENT-CHILD CONNECTION

Before you conclude today's lesson, open your Bible to Mark 2:1–12, and read the story about how Jesus healed a paralytic. Wrap up by saying something like this: "Talk about persistence! These four friends were so concerned about the well-being of their sick buddy, they were willing to drag him onto the roof, tear a hole in it. . .and lower the man right in front of Jesus. They didn't let the challenge of a crowded room stop them. They were persistent with their selfless act."

TALK TO GOD

As you pray, encourage your child to (1) thank Jesus for being with us forever and (2) ask the Lord to help her be part of God's plan.

61

PRINCE OF PEACE

For to us a child is born, to us a son is given, and the government will be on his shoulders. And he will be called Wonderful Counselor, Mighty God, Everlasting Father, Prince of Peace.

Isaiah 9:6

FAMILY QUEST

Roller coasters are fun. Loop, lunge, plunge, zip, flip, whirl—if your stomach can hold up, it's an awesome feeling having your body flung in a zillion directions. But when your life starts to feel this way, that's a different matter! Take a few minutes to dream up the "ultimate" roller-coaster ride. Draw a picture of it.

TALK IT OUT

- Read 2 Corinthians 1:10. Who gives us hope when life begins to feel like a roller-coaster ride?
- In what ways is Jesus the "Prince of Peace"?
- What things help you to feel calm and peaceful?

PARENT-CHILD CONNECTION

Life is like a roller coaster—so many ups and downs can take place in a single day. It's good to let your kids know that this is normal. Help them understand that life often fluctuates between happy moments and stressful ones. But God is always our constant. He is with us no matter what kind of day we are having.

TALK TO GOD

As you pray, encourage your child to (1) thank Jesus for comforting us and (2) ask the Lord for help to trust Him during hardships.

62

PURE

*But we know that when Christ appears,
we shall be like him, for we shall see him as he is.
All who have this hope in him purify themselves, just as he is pure.*

1 JOHN 3:2–3

FAMILY QUEST

Cut an apple into two equal pieces. Soak one half in a water and salt solution for 15 minutes. Allow the other half to be exposed to light. During your family devotion time, stick the apple back together, hiding the inside. Hold it up and say, "Think about this apple as the inside of someone's heart. One side has been polluted by the world; the other has been purified by Jesus." Now expose the inside of the apple.

TALK IT OUT

- Like the brown side of the apple, what kinds of things can make us yucky on the inside?
- Like the side that has been "purified" in salt and water, how does God make us pure? (Examples: prayer, repentance, Bible reading.)
- Read Isaiah 6:5. What gives us confidence to stand before the Lord on judgment day?

PARENT-CHILD CONNECTION

It's easy to see only the bad in the world. But that isn't an accurate picture at all. This is the world that God made. There are signs and reminders of Him everywhere. But it is also broken by sin. Being able to discern between the good and the bad is sometimes difficult. This kind of discernment is the ability you are trying to instill in your child with this exercise.

TALK TO GOD

As you pray, encourage your child to (1) thank Jesus for giving him a clean heart and (2) ask the Lord for help in living a pure life.

63

RIGHTEOUS

*This righteousness is given through
faith in Jesus Christ to all who believe.*
Romans 3:22

FAMILY QUEST

Go online or flip open a book and find a picture of firefighters. Spend some time studying the images, especially the outfits of firefighters. Say something like this: "The Bible tells us that God is holy and pure. And His goodness is so good, it's like a righteous fire that—on judgment day—will burn up everything that is evil and sinful."

TALK IT OUT

- If we are sinners—and the Bible says we are—how can we be saved from what is to come? (Answer: Our faith in Jesus Christ.)
- As the firefighters are made fireproof by their suits, we can be protected through Jesus Christ. He wraps us in His love and holiness. Read Galatians 3:26–27. How does this make you feel?
- Now read Isaiah 64:6. Are we made righteous through good works? Nope. It happens through our faith in Jesus and our relationship with Him.

PARENT-CHILD CONNECTION

God has done the work for us. But we still have to accept it. People come into relationship with God for many different reasons. But once that partnership begins, His righteousness begins to change us from the inside out. This process brings us closer and closer to Him. Good works begin to flow out as our hearts are transformed by our Creator. It is His presence in our lives that makes us righteous.

TALK TO GOD

As you pray, encourage your child to (1) thank Jesus for His love and (2) ask the Lord to build a "right heart" in each one of us.

64

RULER OF ALL THINGS

*"'But you, Bethlehem. . .out of you will come
a ruler who will shepherd my people Israel.'"*
MATTHEW 2:6

FAMILY QUEST

Have each family member dress up like a ruler (robe, scepter, crown, etc.). Take turns playing "Ruler Says" (like you would play Simon Says).

TALK IT OUT

- How did it feel to be a ruler?
- What does a good ruler do? What does a good shepherd do?
- Talk about Jesus' humble birth compared to how most rulers were born in His day.
- How can you allow Jesus to be your Ruler and Shepherd?

PARENT-CHILD CONNECTION

Power can make people do crazy things. As you played this game, you probably noticed the ways that different family members' personalities came out. This is a great chance to talk about how God is different from any other ruler—*ever*! He doesn't abuse His power. Instead, He uses it to save us.

TALK TO GOD

As you pray, encourage your child to (1) thank Jesus for being a good Ruler and Shepherd and (2) ask the Lord to help her follow His leadership every day.

65

SELF-EXISTENT

"Very truly I tell you," Jesus answered,
"before Abraham was born, I am!"
JOHN 8:58

FAMILY QUEST

Have everyone say their birth date and then share their earliest memory.

TALK IT OUT

- Read Exodus 3:13–14. In light of these verses, what does Jesus mean by "I am"?
- Read Psalm 90:2. What does this verse tell us about Jesus?
- Why do you think knowing that Jesus is eternal is important?

PARENT-CHILD CONNECTION

The more we know about God, the more we begin to understand how amazing it is that He wants to include us in His plans. Our Creator lives outside of time. But He invented time so we could have a chance to live our lives. It gives us a chance to pursue Him. Just as we benefit from living within time, we also benefit from a God who is above and beyond our world.

TALK TO GOD

As you pray, encourage your child to (1) thank Jesus for His eternal presence and (2) ask the Lord to help him believe in Jesus with all his heart and mind.

66
SELF-SUFFICIENT

Who has measured the waters in the hollow of his hand, or with the breadth of his hand marked off the heavens? Who has held the dust of the earth in a basket, or weighed the mountains on the scales and the hills in a balance? Who can fathom the Spirit of the LORD, or instruct the LORD as his counselor? Whom did the LORD consult to enlighten him, and who taught him the right way? Who was it that taught him knowledge or showed him the path of understanding?

ISAIAH 40:12–14

FAMILY QUEST

Find three small balls and try to juggle. Unless you are in the minority of people who can juggle, this will be difficult and funny at the same time.

TALK IT OUT

- How long do you think it would take to learn to juggle?
- How can God do so many things at one time?
- Can you list all of the things that God handles by Himself at one time? Does He need help from anyone else?

PARENT-CHILD CONNECTION

This devotional helps us all to see how different we are from God. His abilities and understanding are far beyond anything we humans could ever achieve. And He uses that knowledge to guide us through life. He is powerful and loving. We couldn't ask for a better God!

TALK TO GOD

As you pray, encourage your child to (1) thank Jesus for being so big and mighty and (2) ask the Lord to help him appreciate what He has done for him.

67

SLOW TO ANGER

And he passed in front of Moses, proclaiming,
"The LORD, the LORD, the compassionate and gracious God,
slow to anger, abounding in love and faithfulness."
EXODUS 34:6

FAMILY QUEST

It's showtime! Using stuffed animals, dolls, sock puppets, and your imagination, engage your child in a spontaneous skit about anger. Don't stress—just make up your story on the spot. Scene 1 involves quick-tempered, impatient characters who want what they want *right now*! Scene 2 demonstrates love, selflessness, and the amazing patience of our one and only God whom the Bible describes as "slow to anger."

TALK IT OUT

- Based on our skit, why do you think it's wrong to be quick-tempered?
- When the Bible describes God as "slow to anger," what do you think that means?
- Read Titus 3:3–8. Aren't you happy that God is patient and forgiving?

PARENT-CHILD CONNECTION

Based on the age of your child, this demonstration can get very complex. Younger children will be able to grasp a very basic idea of anger versus patience. But older children will probably have more questions. They may ask, "What if I'm standing up for someone else?" Or "Would God really want us to wait before defending innocent people from bad guys?" Take time to discuss the difference between being angry and being temporarily upset. Anger comes from a deeper place and often does not end well. It is this type of emotion that He is warning us against.

TALK TO GOD

As you pray, encourage your child to (1) thank Jesus for His patience and (2) ask the Lord to teach us to be slow to anger and much more patient with others.

68

SOVEREIGN

*For as the soil makes the sprout come up and a
garden causes seeds to grow, so the Sovereign LORD will
make righteousness and praise spring up before all nations.*
ISAIAH 61:11

FAMILY QUEST

Take a walk in your yard and/or garden and look at all of the
different plants that are growing. If it is wintertime, visit a local nursery
or a botanical garden.

TALK IT OUT

- How do the seeds know how to grow?
- How do we know God controls (through His sovereignty) all of
  creation?
- How is Jesus sovereign over you? Do you see this as a good
  thing? Why?

PARENT-CHILD CONNECTION

God is sovereign even if we do not accept Him as our Savior. Our
understanding, or lack of understanding, does not change the character of
God. It only changes how we see and interact with Him. His sovereignty
is a fact. And He gives us the chance to open our eyes and recognize
Him, or walk through life with blinders on. Encourage your kids to "see"
God in our amazing world.

TALK TO GOD

As you pray, encourage your child to (1) thank Jesus for His power,
control, and creativity and (2) ask the Lord to help her trust in His power.

69

STRONG

*The LORD is my light and my salvation—whom shall I fear? The
LORD is the stronghold of my life—of whom shall I be afraid?*
PSALM 27:1

FAMILY QUEST

Think of the strongest superheroes you can imagine. What makes
them so great? Grab a towel from the bathroom, fasten it on your child's
shoulders, and then instruct him to act out the strength of a superhero.
Take turns being superheroes!

TALK IT OUT

- What made your superhero so strong?
- Why does your favorite hero make you feel so safe?
- Read 1 Corinthians 1:25. God is smarter and stronger than the
  smartest and strongest man who ever lived. How does that make
  you feel?

PARENT-CHILD CONNECTION

Discuss the difference between being afraid and feeling fear. At times,
they can be one and the same. But most of the time, temporary fear may
be able to save us from an unsafe situation. Fear can be a good warning
system. But you can't live your entire life being afraid. Well. . .you can,
but you really don't want to. And God doesn't want you to. He is our
mighty God and He wants what is best for us.

TALK TO GOD

As you pray, encourage your child to (1) thank Jesus for keeping us
safe and (2) ask the Lord to give us strength when we feel weak.

70

SUSTAINER OF ALL CREATION

For in him all things were created: things in heaven and on earth,
visible and invisible, whether thrones or powers or rulers or
authorities; all things have been created through him and for him.
He is before all things, and in him all things hold together.

COLOSSIANS 1:16–17

FAMILY QUEST

Build two identical houses out of craft sticks. Glue one of them together but leave the other unglued. Discuss how God created our world and continues to hold it together.

TALK IT OUT

- Which house would be better to live in?
- Did God's work end after He created the world? What is God's work today?
- Does He ever leave us?

PARENT-CHILD CONNECTION

Likely your child will ask, "If God can keep everything together, then why do things fall apart sometimes?" And this is a very good question. This is a good time to discuss "free will." Because we live in a world where humans get to make choices, they will sometimes make poor decisions. Because of this brokenness, our world doesn't always work the way God wishes. But instead of making everyone follow Him, He gives us the choice. We can trust that He always wants the best for us.

TALK TO GOD

As you pray, encourage your child to (1) thank Jesus for creating such an amazing world and for holding it together, and (2) ask the Lord to help him recognize the many ways He helps him every day.

71
THREE-IN-ONE

As soon as Jesus was baptized, he went up out of the water.
At that moment heaven was opened, and he saw the Spirit of
God descending like a dove and alighting on him. And a voice from
heaven said, "This is my Son, whom I love; with him I am well pleased."
MATTHEW 3:16–17

FAMILY QUEST

Conduct an experiment in the kitchen. Examine the three forms of H_2O. First, hold and study an ice cube. Then place your hands under running water. Third, watch the mist of steam as it rises from a pan of boiling water (from a safe distance, of course). Now think of the Trinity: the Father, the Son, and the Holy Spirit. God doesn't just take on three different forms; He is all three Persons at the same time. Amazing!

TALK IT OUT
- How can God be all three Persons at the same time?
- Which Person is here on earth with us right now?
- How would you explain the Trinity to someone?

PARENT-CHILD CONNECTION

There is no specific passage in scripture that uses the word *Trinity*. But the idea is woven throughout the Word. God even speaks of Himself in the plural during the creation story in Genesis 1–3. There is no simple way to explain the Trinity other than to recognize that God is multifaceted and possesses capabilities beyond our understanding. We can all rejoice that He has chosen to reveal His three Persons for our benefit.

TALK TO GOD

As you pray, encourage your child to (1) thank Jesus for letting us talk directly to Him just as we do with other friends and (2) ask the Lord to give us the courage to take any questions we have directly to Him.

72

TRUSTWORTHY

Trust in the LORD forever, for the LORD,
the LORD himself, is the Rock eternal.
ISAIAH 26:4

FAMILY QUEST

Find a safe, comfortable, spot in your house. Sit or stand about three feet behind your child. Then have her close her eyes, cross her hands across her waist, and fall directly into your arms. This act of trust may come hard even to a young child.

TALK IT OUT

- Was it hard to just drop without bracing your fall? How did you feel?
- Is it easy to trust? Why or why not?
- What are some of the things about God that make Him trustworthy?

PARENT-CHILD CONNECTION

Some kids are more trusting than others. This quick exercise can tell you a lot about how your child sees the world. You can now shape your conversations with this new information. This is an opportunity to help your child begin to see God as the One who is trustworthy in all situations.

TALK TO GOD

As you pray, encourage your child to (1) thank Jesus for His dependability and (2) ask the Lord to help her trust God.

73

UNCHANGING

*"I the LORD do not change. So you, the descendants of Jacob,
are not destroyed. Ever since the time of your ancestors you
have turned away from my decrees and have not kept them.
Return to me, and I will return to you," says the LORD Almighty.*
MALACHI 3:6–7

FAMILY QUEST

Take a walk with your child. Notice the things that change often and the things that don't change or seldom change. Keep track of each type and see whether you find more things that change or more things that don't change.

TALK IT OUT

- What does Malachi 3:6–7 tell us about God?
- If God never changes, what does that tell you about how God will respond to you? Your family?
- How does the unchangeableness of God make you feel?

PARENT-CHILD CONNECTION

Help your child to connect God with her world. It's great if a flower reminds her of God creating our world. It's wonderful if the changing of the seasons helps her to understand that there are seasons in life. A mountain can be a reminder that God is our solid rock. The more ways you can help your child connect God with her world, the more she will begin to see that God is a part of her everyday life.

TALK TO GOD

As you pray, encourage your child to (1) thank Jesus for His never-changing love for her and (2) ask the Lord to help her know that He is always with her.

74

THE WAY, THE TRUTH, AND THE LIFE

*Jesus answered, "I am the way and the truth and the life.
No one comes to the Father except through me."*
JOHN 14:6

FAMILY QUEST

Read John 14:5–14. Emphasize that committing our lives to Jesus Christ is the only way to live with Him in heaven. Make sure your child understands that Jesus and God are one. Next, have your child write a short note, thanking Jesus for being our way to the heavenly Father.

TALK IT OUT

- How many ways are there to the Father?
- How do we learn what's true? (Answer: By reading the Bible.)
- How is Jesus the Way? The Truth? The Life?

PARENT-CHILD CONNECTION

Identifying Jesus as the one true way is significant. Your kids live in the same world as we adults. We know there are many voices out there that make very different claims about who we are and who God is. Children are very impressionable. They take in a lot of information as they begin to form their worldview. The key is not to lock them away from the world. The best approach is to discuss God's true identity in an open and honest environment. This will help your kids to discern new information as they move forward in life.

TALK TO GOD

As you pray, encourage your child to (1) thank Jesus for making it possible to come to the Father and (2) ask the Lord to help him live for God his entire life.

75

WONDERFUL

Sing to him, sing praise to him;
tell of all his wonderful acts.
PSALM 105:2

FAMILY QUEST

Lead your child in a "Family Sing-a-Rama." Make it festive! Blow up balloons and wear party hats. Pull out some musical instruments and sing songs that celebrate the *wonder* of our *wondrous, wonderful* God!

TALK IT OUT

- The Bible describes God as wonderful. Can you think of some things that make Him wonderful?
- What's the biggest, most wonderful thing God has done for those who commit their hearts to Him?
- How do you think the Lord feels when we praise Him?

PARENT-CHILD CONNECTION

The Bible tells us that heaven rejoices every time someone accepts Jesus as their Savior. This is the same type of celebration we should be offering up to God. He has given us the amazing gift of salvation. He paid the price for us to spend eternity with Him. Now that's a reason to celebrate!

TALK TO GOD

As you pray, encourage your child to (1) thank Jesus for all the wonderful things He does for us and (2) ask the Lord to fill her heart with joy as she thinks of the ways that God has blessed her.

76

WORTHY OF ALL HONOR AND GLORY

"You are worthy, our Lord and God, to receive glory and honor and power, for you created all things, and by your will they were created and have their being."
REVELATION 4:11

FAMILY QUEST

Take turns naming your hero. Explain both their strong and weak points. Now discuss how God is far more worthy of your praise than anything or any person He created.

TALK IT OUT

- What does it mean to be worthy of glory?
- How is God bigger and better than your hero?
- How can we honor God this week as a family?

PARENT-CHILD CONNECTION

Honor is not a word that is used very much today. As you discuss this word, help your child to find practical ways he can honor God. Honor goes far beyond just following the rules. It is a matter of the heart. It's like singing a praise song at church. It doesn't mean anything if we just sing the words without meaning them. But when the words come from the heart, God is pleased with our honest praise. This example might help your child see the difference between following the rules and following God with his heart.

TALK TO GOD

As you pray, encourage your child to (1) thank Jesus for being his hero and (2) ask the Lord to help him praise Him.

Part Three

My Faith in God

He Gives Me. . .

11

ACCEPTANCE

*"I will be a Father to you, and you will be my
sons and daughters, says the Lord Almighty."*
2 CORINTHIANS 6:18

FAMILY QUEST

Dig through an album and find some pictures of you and your child the day you brought him home from the hospital. Point to yourself in the picture. Talk about how proud you look and how happy and proud you still are to have him as your son.

TALK IT OUT

- In what ways is God like your father?
- How does God make you part of His family? (Read John 1:12.)
- How does knowing you're part of God's family make your life better?

PARENT-CHILD CONNECTION

Kids have a limited view of what it means to be a family. If you ask them to explain what a family is, they will most likely describe their own. Some may include the family of a friend or neighbor. But they don't know the complexities that influence the structures of families in different cultures. So it's important to remember your child's perspective when explaining that we are a part of God's family. They can't help but relate it to their own understanding of family.

TALK TO GOD

As you pray, encourage your child to (1) thank God for accepting him as part of His family and (2) ask the Lord to help him become more and more pleasing to God his heavenly Father.

78

CHOICES TO MAKE

*"Enter through the narrow gate. For wide is the gate and broad is
the road that leads to destruction, and many enter through it. But small
is the gate and narrow the road that leads to life, and only a few find it."*
MATTHEW 7:13–14

FAMILY QUEST

Play a little game of chance. Think up a number between 1 and
100,000,000 and write it on a slip of paper. Have your child try to guess
the number. It will probably be very hard for her to guess it correctly.
Then think up a different number between 1 and 5. There is a much
higher chance of her guessing correctly.

TALK IT OUT

- Why was it so much harder to guess the number when it was
  between 1 and 100,000,000? Why was it easier when there were
  only five numbers to guess from?
- We have a lot of choices to make in life. Is it always easy to know
  which ones are correct?
- Do you ever feel overwhelmed by so many choices? Why is it
  important to make good decisions?
- How is this like following God? Which choices could you make
  that would make a difference in your faith life?
- Reread Matthew 7:13–14 and discuss why these choices are
  important to God.

PARENT-CHILD CONNECTION

Fortunately, we don't have to guess about God. This idea of walking on a narrow road can be intimidating. But it doesn't have to be since God is the One who helps us down the path. We don't have to take a chance and hope it turns out well. We just have to trust that He will show us the way. The sooner your kids figure this out, the more hopeful they will be about their future.

TALK TO GOD

As you pray, encourage your child to (1) thank Jesus for giving us a pathway to Him and (2) ask the Lord to help her make good choices in life that are pleasing to God.

79

COMFORT

*For God is not a God
of disorder but of peace.*
1 CORINTHIANS 14:33

FAMILY QUEST

Pick out your favorite things. Maybe it's a warm fuzzy blanket, ice cream, a funny cartoon, or a comfy sweatshirt. Take a few minutes to discuss why you selected your item.

TALK IT OUT

- Why did you pick the item you chose?
- How does this item make you feel when you've had a long, busy day?
- How is God our comforter? How does He make you feel at the end of a long busy day?
- Does He really care about our small problems?
- Do you regularly ask Him for comfort when you are feeling troubled or scared?

PARENT-CHILD CONNECTION

Kids feel safe when there are boundaries and order in life. They may push back, resist, or try to find a way around your boundaries. But they also find comfort in knowing they are there. As our Comforter, God has given us parameters in our lives. He gives us order for our own benefit. Help your child to understand that God always works for our well-being. He is on our side!

TALK TO GOD

As you pray, encourage your child to (1) thank God for loving every one of us and (2) ask the Lord to help him ask God for help in times of trouble.

80

CREATIVITY

In the beginning God created the heavens and the earth.
GENESIS 1:1

FAMILY QUEST

Place several craft items on your kitchen table: finger paints, construction paper, glitter, crayons, clay—anything that will get your child's creative juices flowing. Set a timer and say this: "Create a work of art for _____ [name of friend or relative]. Use your imagination and have fun!"

TALK IT OUT

- How did your child come up with her creation?
- What came easy? What was hard?
- Say this: "God gives us the ability to use our imaginations. In what ways is the Lord creative?" (Answer: He created all things.)

PARENT-CHILD CONNECTION

All creativity flows from God. He is the original source of all we know. And we were created in His image. Therefore, He totally expects us to use our own creativity in our lives. Help your kids to find ways to explore new ideas as they explore their world. Just imagine how we can impact our culture with new and exciting ways to show others God's love.

TALK TO GOD

As you pray, encourage your child to (1) thank Jesus for giving her a good imagination and the ability to be creative, and (2) ask the Lord to help her use her abilities for Him.

81

DELIVERANCE

*Because he himself suffered when he was tempted,
he is able to help those who are being tempted.*
HEBREWS 2:18

FAMILY QUEST

Tell a story from your childhood about being tempted to do something bad. Make it simple so a young child can relate to it. Then explain how each person is tempted in life. Adults and children are often faced with difficult decisions. Temptation is something we all share. Even Jesus was tempted.

TALK IT OUT

- Does God get upset with us when we are tempted?
- What's the difference between being tempted and making a wrong decision?
- Why do you think Jesus was tempted?
- Do you think He understands what we are thinking when we are faced with temptation?

PARENT-CHILD CONNECTION

A lot of people feel guilty when they face temptation. But freedom comes with the realization that we all are tempted. We run into problems when we give in to temptation. Letting your child know that temptation is a normal part of life will help him better face tough decisions.

TALK TO GOD

As you pray, encourage your child to (1) thank Jesus for being our example and (2) ask the Lord to help him always remember that God is our biggest fan and wants to deliver us from bad decisions.

82

FORGIVENESS

*Bear with each other and forgive one another if any of you
has a grievance against someone. Forgive as the Lord forgave you.*
COLOSSIANS 3:13

FAMILY QUEST

Retell Luke 15:11–32, the parable of the prodigal son. Make it a dramatic reading or a skit that involves the whole family. (Assign roles and act out the story.) Next, tell how we are all prodigals (wayward, rebellious) yet loved by our heavenly Father and forgiven when we return to Him.

TALK IT OUT

- The father in Luke 15:11–32 showed love and forgiveness to his son when he returned home. How does this make you feel?
- How are we like the prodigal son?
- Colossians 3:13 instructs us to "forgive as the Lord forgave you." Why is it important for us to forgive others?

PARENT-CHILD CONNECTION

This story offers far more than the tale of one rebellious son. There are other characters to whom we can relate. There is the father who loves his son no matter his behavior. He freely welcomes him back with a big celebration. And there is the brother who stayed home and performed his duties with diligence. He is also the one who was offended when his rebel brother was embraced upon his return. Most kids will quickly identify with one of these men. And lessons can be learned from each one. Discuss the attributes and struggles of each character with your child.

TALK TO GOD

As you pray, encourage your child to (1) thank Jesus for His forgiveness and (2) ask, "Is there someone I need to forgive?" Ask the Lord for help to forgive others.

83

FREEDOM

Jesus replied, "Very truly I tell you,
everyone who sins is a slave to sin. . . .
So if the Son sets you free, you will be free indeed."
JOHN 8:34–36

FAMILY QUEST

Tell your kids about a time you did something and knew it was not pleasing to God. Then ask if they have done something they wished they hadn't done—something they felt was wrong. Explain that Jesus sets us free by forgiving what we did wrong and helping us not to do it again.

TALK IT OUT

- How can we become "slaves" to doing wrong things?
- How does it make you feel to know that Jesus can give you freedom from doing wrong?
- What is one thing you'd like to *not* do again?

PARENT-CHILD CONNECTION

God offers us freedom. Even when we mess up, He will forgive us. When we choose to try to live without His guidance, we will get off track and fall short of the life we were meant to live. When we try to manipulate the truth for our own benefit, we become slaves to our twisted ways. The only path to freedom is by the mercy of God. Using examples of how sin drags us down is the best way to explain to your kids that the better alternative is to trust God and His ways.

TALK TO GOD

As you pray, encourage your child to (1) thank Jesus for giving us freedom in Him and (2) ask the Lord to help her be free from sinful actions.

84

GOD'S WILL

*Do not conform to the pattern of this world, but be transformed by
the renewing of your mind. Then you will be able to test and approve
what God's will is—his good, pleasing and perfect will.*
ROMANS 12:2

FAMILY QUEST

Before you start this lesson, get a children's book that illustrates
different occupations. Spend this session talking about jobs, plans for
the future. . .and God. Flip through the book and examine photos of
different professions. Say this: "When you grow up, you can accomplish
anything you put your mind to. But it's important that we do exactly
what God wants us to do."

TALK IT OUT

- How do we figure out what God wants us to do? (Answer: By
  praying, talking to mature Christian believers like our pastor, and
  reading the Bible.)
- Why is Bible reading an important way to learn what God
  wants?
- Why must we put God's will first—before what we want?

PARENT-CHILD CONNECTION

Sometimes it's difficult to know God's will. We get overwhelmed by
our options and ask too many "what if" questions. Thinking about our
future can be exciting. Or it can be stressful. Help your kids to know that
we don't have to have all the answers. Doing God's will begins with doing
what we already know to do. We are to pursue God through prayer, Bible
reading, and obedience to the Spirit. Through this process, He will guide

us day by day. That is what God wants from us.

TALK TO GOD

As you pray, encourage your child to: (1) thank Jesus for the special things He wants him to do in life and (2) ask the Lord to help him to always seek God first.

85

A HOME IN HEAVEN

Surely your goodness and love will follow me all the days of my life,
and I will dwell in the house of the LORD forever.
PSALM 23:6

FAMILY QUEST

Find a quiet and cozy place to be still. Have everyone close their eyes and picture their favorite place. Take a little imaginary trip as you pretend that you have been away on a long journey. Then describe how you felt when you finally returned to your favorite place. Talk about your excitement, joy, relief, and peace when you arrived. Then have your children do the same.

TALK IT OUT

- Is it possible to get excited about a place you have never been before? Like heaven?
- Who gets to go to heaven? Will your family and friends be there?
- What are some wrong ideas the world has about heaven? How does this compare to how the Bible describes it?
- How does your view of heaven change the way you live? Do you daydream about it? Do you get excited about spending your future there?

PARENT-CHILD CONNECTION

It's hard to get excited about heaven if you don't know anything about it. Movies and television shows sometimes offer a warped view of who will be in heaven and what it will be like once you are there. Take some time to read about heaven in the Bible. Help your child to discern the difference between the truth (the Bible) and someone's fantasy of heaven. This will help her get excited about her future.

TALK TO GOD

As you pray, encourage your child to (1) thank Jesus for preparing a place for her in heaven and (2) ask the Lord to help her live for Him now.

86

HOPE

For you have been my hope, Sovereign LORD, my confidence since my youth.
PSALM 71:5

FAMILY QUEST

Create a game: Make a list of things that people hope for (money, safety, toys, trips, fame, knowledge, success, etc.). Cut the list up and place the slips of paper in a bowl. Take turns pulling one slip out of the bowl and reading it out loud. That person then gives his opinion as to whether he hopes for that item. After you have all taken a turn, everyone can take turns adding to this list.

TALK IT OUT

- How does hope change the way we live?
- Where does your hope come from?
- How is God our hope?
- How is wishing for something different from having hope?

PARENT-CHILD CONNECTION

There is a significant difference between placing our hope in God and merely wishing for good things in our lives. God is not a genie in a bottle. Instead, He is always looking out for us. But He does it by using His unending knowledge and wisdom. He offers us so much more than anything we could ever wish for. It is in this truth that we can all find hope. It is a hope based on God and His love.

TALK TO GOD

As you pray, encourage your child to (1) thank Jesus for his future and (2) ask the Lord to help him recognize the important things in life.

87

JOY

*May the God of hope fill you with
all joy and peace as you trust in him.*
ROMANS 15:13

FAMILY QUEST

Draw three large circles. List things that bring you *joy* in the left circle and things that give you *peace* in the one on the right. Fill the middle circle with words that fit both categories.

TALK IT OUT

- What does *joy* mean? How is it different from *peace*?
- How is having joy in your heart different from feeling happy?
- Do you think you can get this joy and hope anywhere other than God?

PARENT-CHILD CONNECTION

The exercise above is probably very familiar to most elementary-age kids. It is used in most classrooms to help children identify the different elements of a story and distinguish how they are connected to one another. Hopefully, God and the things of God will be listed in your middle circle. Help your child see how God brings both peace and joy through His many blessings.

TALK TO GOD

As you pray, encourage your child to (1) thank Jesus for wanting her to have joy and (2) ask the Lord to help her have peace in her heart.

88

PEACE

*For he himself is our peace, who has made the two groups one
and has destroyed the barrier, the dividing wall of hostility.*

EPHESIANS 2:14

FAMILY QUEST

Using toy soldiers, stuffed animals, and blocks, play a game that drives home the message about peace. Set up two warring tribes and place a wall between them. Retell Ephesians 2:11–18. Emphasize that Jesus destroyed a "dividing wall of hostility" between God and us. Break down the wall together, explaining that Jesus has given us peace. . .and eternal life with Him!

TALK IT OUT

- How is sin like a big wall between God and us?
- How did Jesus destroy that wall?
- Read Colossians 3:15. How do we let the peace of Christ rule in our hearts?
- Is there anyone you need to make peace with?

PARENT-CHILD CONNECTION

Some kids may have a difficult time understanding the symbolism of a "dividing wall." If your child is more of a literal thinker, help him to imagine a physical wall that divides us from God. The Family Quest above will help with this. But if your child's mind is already full of word pictures, help him identify some of the ways that we humans can build the walls that divide. But most of all, conclude your conversation by reassuring your child that God is our Lord of peace. It doesn't matter how big, wide, strong, or long the walls are that divide us from Him because He can overcome them all. He can give us the only true peace!

TALK TO GOD

As you pray, encourage your child to (1) thank Jesus for giving each of us peace with God and (2) ask the Lord to help us live in peace with others.

89

PRAYER

Devote yourselves to prayer,
being watchful and thankful.
COLOSSIANS 4:2

FAMILY QUEST

Using pretend phones, have three fun conversations with your child: (1) a *Jabber Fest*—the two of you talk over each other. . .with nobody listening; (2) a *One-Sided Sling*—you do all the talking, never giving your child a chance to respond; and (3) a *Silly Sing-a-Thon*—your kid sings his or her conversation, using disjointed lines that don't make sense.

TALK IT OUT

- Did any of this make sense? Did we have a meaningful conversation?
- If our hearts aren't into what we're saying, our prayers can be this way. (Discuss specific examples with your child.) How does this make God feel?
- James 5:13–15 gives us some great clues about prayer. Based on these verses, what is prayer, and how does God want us to do it?

PARENT-CHILD CONNECTION

Kids learn to communicate from an early age. Cries turn into words, words turn into sentences, sentences turn into conversations, and so on. A child's need to interact and be heard drives this natural development. But we all need a little more help when it comes to prayer. Yes, we all have a deep-seated need to know God. And anyone, anywhere, can cry out to Him. But a strong prayer life is taught. As parents, take the time to teach your kids how to pray. The examples above will help them understand the need to connect with God in this way. But the basics of praise, thankfulness, petition, confession, and silence before the Lord are disciplines that must be practiced. And you, Mom and Dad, are your kids' role models. Pray with them as you help them to develop this fundamental spiritual practice.

TALK TO GOD

As you pray, encourage your child to (1) thank Jesus for the gift of prayer and (2) ask the Lord to show us how to pray.

90

PURPOSE

For we are God's handiwork, created in Christ Jesus to do
good works, which God prepared in advance for us to do.
EPHESIANS 2:10

FAMILY QUEST

Go shopping with your child. Together, pick out items that you can give to a homeless shelter or donate to a church food drive: socks, undergarments, canned foods, toiletries, etc. Go together as you hand over these items to the charity of your choice.

TALK IT OUT

- The Bible tells us that we are "God's workmanship, created in Christ Jesus to do good works." How is giving things to those in need a good work?
- What are some other things God wants us to do for Him and for others?
- The Lord gives us all a purpose to fulfill during our lives. What does this mean? Why is it important to live for His purpose—and not our own?

PARENT-CHILD CONNECTION

Most kids know that it is honorable to do good deeds. But kids also need to know that God created us to live together in community. Helping each other out is built into who we were created to be. We all have talents that can be used for God's glory. Somewhere right now someone is praying to God for a little extra help. You can be the person who is their answer to prayer. Your talent may be what is needed. Or maybe the donation of some of your possessions can change someone's life. Create an environment of giving as you model compassion and caring.

TALK TO GOD

As you pray, encourage your child to (1) thank Jesus for giving us all an important purpose in life and (2) ask the Lord to help each family member discover what God wants them to do.

91

A RELATIONSHIP WITH HIM

"Here I am! I stand at the door and knock. If anyone hears my voice and opens the door, I will come in and eat with that person, and they with me."
REVELATION 3:20

FAMILY QUEST

Pull out markers, crayons, and paper. Instruct your child to draw a picture of himself playing with his best friend. At the bottom of the paper, help him write three things he likes most about his friend. (Plan on giving the artwork to your child's friend.)

TALK IT OUT

- What do you enjoy doing most with your friend? (Encourage your child to talk about his picture and articulate why he likes the person he drew.)
- When we're friends with people, we have a *relationship* with them. What does the word *relationship* mean?
- What does it mean to have a relationship with Jesus? In what ways is He our best friend?

PARENT-CHILD CONNECTION

Everyone needs to be wanted. We all get excited when someone goes out of their way to get to know us. As we read in the Bible, God wants to know us. He wants us to want Him as much as He wants us. He is the best Friend any of us could ever have. All we have to do is accept His friendship. It's good for your child to know that he is wanted by the King of kings!

TALK TO GOD

As you pray, encourage your child to (1) thank Jesus for being his best Friend and (2) ask the Lord to deepen his relationship with Him.

92

RESCUE

*Because he himself suffered when he was tempted,
he is able to help those who are being tempted.*
HEBREWS 2:18

FAMILY QUEST

Play a game of Pass or Tell. Write down several different scenarios that include temptations. For example, "You are in a store and your friend wants you to steal a bag of chips. What do you do?" Cut them out and place them in a hat. Have each person pull out a scenario and read it out loud. Then that person must answer how she would handle the situation. You can even include some of the times you have been tempted in life.

TALK IT OUT

- Is everyone tempted? How often?
- How does Jesus rescue you when you are tempted?
- How do we know what God wants us to do? (Read 1 Corinthians 10:13.)

PARENT-CHILD CONNECTION

Kids love to learn new things about their parents. The game and discussion above have the potential for a great interaction between you and your kids. Try not to make them feel like they are being tested. You want them to speak freely and ask questions. Help them to know that God is always ready to rescue them from any mistake or difficult situation.

TALK TO GOD

As you pray, encourage your child to (1) thank God for rescuing her when she's tempted to do wrong and (2) ask the Lord to help her know that she doesn't face anything that He can't help her with.

93

RESTORATION

He refreshes my soul. He guides me along the right paths for his name's sake.
PSALM 23:3

FAMILY QUEST

Take an old vase or some "white elephant" item in your house that is breakable. Go outside and smash it on the ground. Collect the pieces and then try to reassemble the item piece by piece.

TALK IT OUT

- Were you able to put the broken item back together again? Did it look the same?
- How can you be broken?
- Do you ever have to ask God to put you back together?
- Are you useful to God after He has put you back together?

PARENT-CHILD CONNECTION

God restores us to a condition that is better than anything we could imagine. Sometimes we only want small fixes in life while He desires that we live a full and complete life. He wants us to be more than just functional; He wants us to share in His mission and passion and calls us to be an integral part of His plan. He continues to do this good work in us every day. He is constantly healing us and restoring us to wholeness. Let your child know that God is our ultimate Healer!

TALK TO GOD

As you pray, encourage your child to (1) thank Jesus for having the power to make him whole again and (2) ask the Lord to restore him and guide him along right paths for His glory.

94

SALVATION

He has saved us and called us to a holy life—not because of anything we have done but because of his own purpose and grace. This grace was given us in Christ Jesus before the beginning of time, but it has now been revealed through the appearing of our Savior, Christ Jesus, who has destroyed death and has brought life and immortality to light through the gospel.

2 TIMOTHY 1:9–10

FAMILY QUEST

Have everyone in the family name their favorite "superhero" and describe a time when their hero saved someone's life. Why did they remember that particular "salvation"?

TALK IT OUT

- How can Jesus save you?
- What is He saving you from?
- Can anyone else save you from evil?
- How can you help others be saved?

PARENT-CHILD CONNECTION

Even children know that the world isn't fair. Sometimes the good guys don't win. Other times we get things we don't deserve. And even if kids don't fully understand it, they know that we live in a broken world. This brokenness separates us from God. He is so pure and clean that He cannot be in union with those who are not. And since we live in this world, there is no way we can be holy through our own power. So we need His forgiveness and salvation in order to be right with Him. And it is this salvation that He offers to us. He has already paid the price. Help your child to know that the salvation God offers is the only true way to be whole and happy.

TALK TO GOD

As you pray, encourage your child to (1) thank Jesus for coming to earth to bring salvation and (2) ask the Lord to forgive her for her sins.

95

A SECOND CHANCE

*One of the high priest's servants. . .challenged him,
"Didn't I see you with him in the garden?" Again Peter denied it.*
JOHN 18:26–27

FAMILY QUEST

Position a wastebasket across the room. Instruct your child to throw a soft ball into the basket. (Tip: Make it impossible to complete this task the first time.) Give him a second chance. . .a third. . .and so on. With each attempt, make reaching the goal easier.

TALK IT OUT

- How did you feel when I gave you a second chance. . .and a third chance?
- Did you know that God gives us second chances too? Listen to how He helped Peter start again. (Read John 18:25–27; 21:15–19.)
- How does it make you feel to know that God gives us a fresh start?

PARENT-CHILD CONNECTION

Too many kids mistakenly believe that the Lord doesn't want them to be honest about their secrets and struggles. They think He will be upset if they tell Him about the bad things they've thought or done. But if God already knows everything about us, even our secret sins can't make Him stop loving us. Tell your child this: "Our Lord is the God of second chances! He wants you to experience His love, forgiveness, and power in *all* areas of your life. Pour out your heart to Him. Share the bad stuff you've thought or done—that's called confession—and He will forgive you."

TALK TO GOD

As you pray, encourage your child to (1) thank Jesus for giving us a second chance and (2) ask the Lord to help him live in a way that pleases Him.

96

SECURITY

In peace I will lie down and sleep,
for you alone, LORD, make me dwell in safety.
PSALM 4:8

FAMILY QUEST

We all need a place we can go to rest and know that everything's going to be okay. Spend some time talking about safe places: our homes, churches, schools.

TALK IT OUT

- What makes a safe place *safe*?
- How does Jesus comfort us and help us feel safe?
- Read Philippians 4:6–7. Talk about God's solution for worrying.

PARENT-CHILD CONNECTION

We try to find security in many things. We protect our children from the bad guys by watching over them and providing them with a safe home. We depend on home security systems, cell phones, 911, teachers, the police, churches, and many other systems in our lives. And these are good people and organizations who care for others. But they can never offer the complete and eternal security of God. He is the only One who can bring peace into our hearts. He is the only One who offers us an eternity in heaven. Teach your kids to seek Him—the only path to real security.

TALK TO GOD

As you pray, encourage your child to (1) thank Jesus for giving us safe places and safe people and (2) ask the Lord to help us pray when we feel scared or worried.

97

STRENGTH

"So do not fear, for I am with you; do not be dismayed, for I am your God. I will strengthen you and help you; I will uphold you with my righteous right hand."
ISAIAH 41:10

FAMILY QUEST

Challenge your child to a tug-of-war competition. It's you versus her. First, mark the floor (preferably a carpeted area) with tape. Then hand the end of a rope to your child. The competition begins. . .and ends with you overpowering her. Next, call in the troops. Invite your spouse (and other children) to help your child. This time they overpower you.

TALK IT OUT

- During round one, why did I win?
- During round two, what gave you strength?
- How does God give us strength when life gets hard?

PARENT-CHILD CONNECTION

Tell your child this: "Spiritual weakness and constant struggles with issues that God says are off-limits—such as lying, cheating, stealing, behaving rudely, acting selfish—are almost always symptoms of a bigger problem in our lives. The *real problem* is often a *heart problem*. And the only way to fix a mixed-up, sin-filled heart is by having a daily truth encounter. That means *spending time in the Word and in prayer*. If we combine Bible reading with prayer, we have a powerful weapon—an invisible sword, so to speak—that can fend off any deception and defeat any struggle that threatens to trap us. This is ultimate strength training!"

TALK TO GOD

As you pray, encourage your child to (1) thank Jesus for giving her strength when she is weak and (2) ask the Lord to walk with her through hard times.

98

UNDERSTANDING

As a father has compassion on his children,
so the LORD has compassion on those who fear him;
for he knows how we are formed, he remembers that we are dust.
PSALM 103:13–14

FAMILY QUEST

Try watching a television show or movie that's in a different language. Turn off all closed-captioning and subtitles and see if you can follow the story line.

TALK IT OUT

- What does God understand about us?
- How does understanding someone influence our attitude toward that person?
- Why does God understand you better than anyone else ever could?

PARENT-CHILD CONNECTION

During today's lesson, impart some practical advice that your children will be able to use all throughout their lives. Whenever they encounter a passage of scripture or Christian doctrine that they don't understand, encourage them to take these two steps: (1) *Ask God for His wisdom and direction*, and then (2) *research the passage*. Explain that the Holy Spirit can guide and direct us in various ways but doesn't usually provide concrete information about a subject. Therefore, we must do the hard work of research alongside the Spirit's subtler guidance. How we research a confusing passage or unclear theology depends on the particular issue we don't understand. Sometimes we should talk to a trusted expert, such as a pastor or a Christian teacher. Sometimes we must head to the library and study a book by a Christian author. However, use caution when doing Google searches and pulling information off the Internet. Make sure the site you visit is trustworthy.

TALK TO GOD

As you pray, encourage your child to (1) thank Jesus for His love and understanding and (2) ask the Lord to help him better understand other people.

99

VICTORY

Brothers and sisters, I do not consider myself yet to have taken hold of it.
But one thing I do: Forgetting what is behind and straining toward
what is ahead, I press on toward the goal to win the prize for
which God has called me heavenward in Christ Jesus.

PHILIPPIANS 3:13–14

FAMILY QUEST

It's game time. Invite the whole family to join you for "Family Faith Olympics." If you're outdoors, and if you have space, create an obstacle course or mark a spot for a relay race. If you're indoors, pull out some age-appropriate board games. After the competition, pass out prizes and congratulate your Olympians.

TALK IT OUT

- What is the prize that God wants us to win?
- Read Romans 8:35–37. How does Jesus help us be conquerors?
- How can we help others to have victory in Jesus?

PARENT-CHILD CONNECTION

As you teach today's lesson, emphasize that the Christian journey is a lot like an Olympic competition. We identify ourselves with Christ, we train spiritually, we discipline our hearts and our minds, and we press ahead with our "eyes on the prize"—eternity with God. At times the competition is thrilling, and at other moments it's downright grueling. Life gets turbulent, and continuing seems too painful, too hard—utterly impossible. (Maybe we're consumed with doubts or a nagging fear or a deep-rooted insecurity.) So when life overwhelms us, how can we stay in the competition? By shifting our focus from the challenge we face to the sufficiency of our Coach: Jesus Christ. Say this: "Let's open our Bibles and read all of Hebrews 11 for a thorough understanding of what an iron-willed commitment is all about." Then emphasize these verses from Hebrews 12: "Let us throw off everything that hinders and the sin that so easily entangles. And let us run with perseverance the race marked out for us, fixing our eyes on Jesus, the pioneer and perfecter of faith. For the joy set before him he endured the cross, scorning its shame, and sat down at the right hand of the throne of God. Consider him who endured such opposition from sinners, so that you will not grow weary and lose heart" (verses 1–3).

TALK TO GOD

As you pray, encourage your child to (1) thank Jesus for giving His people victory in Him and (2) ask the Lord to help you all stay focused on Him and the prize He has for you.

100

WISDOM

*"Therefore everyone who hears these words of mine and puts them
into practice is like a wise man who built his house on the rock."*
MATTHEW 7:24

FAMILY QUEST

Launch a building project using clay. . .and uncooked spaghetti.
Instruct your child to create a tower using these materials. Position
her creation in the middle of a beach towel. The project is timed: she
must finish the building project within ten minutes—and the taller
the structure, the better. Also issue a warning: "An earthquake will test
the strength of your creation!"

TALK IT OUT

- When the time is up, start the earthquake. Tug on one end of the
  towel and test the strength of the structure. Discuss: What made
  your tower strong or weak?
- A good foundation is important, especially when it comes to our
  faith in God. How can we have a "good foundation"?
- Why is it wise to build the foundation of our faith on the "rock"
  of Jesus?

PARENT-CHILD CONNECTION

During this lesson, explain that wisdom, faith, truth, and life
itself come from God. Yet spiritual growth doesn't happen through
mechanical rituals or by filling our minds with "correct theology." It's
nurtured through a Person—Jesus Christ. It is our relationship and daily
walk with Him that will help us grow in wisdom. Therefore, we must be
followers of Jesus, learners of Him. We must be committed to knowing

Him better each day. Our faith grows as we encounter Jesus in the Bible. The message of scripture is the message of Jesus who said, "I am the way and the truth and the life" (John 14:6). Share these additional verses:

- "Consequently, faith comes from hearing the message, and the message is heard through the word about Christ" (Romans 10:17).
- "Do not conform to the pattern of this world, but be transformed by the renewing of your mind. Then you will be able to test and approve what God's will is—his good, pleasing and perfect will" (Romans 12:2).
- "But as for you, continue in what you have learned and have become convinced of, because you know those from whom you learned it, and how from infancy you have known the Holy Scriptures, which are able to make you wise for salvation through faith in Christ Jesus. All Scripture is God-breathed and is useful for teaching, rebuking, correcting and training in righteousness, so that the servant of God may be thoroughly equipped for every good work" (2 Timothy 3:14–17).

TALK TO GOD

As you pray, encourage your child to (1) thank Jesus for giving each one of us wisdom and (2) ask the Lord to help him make wise choices.

101

THE WORD OF GOD

For the word of God is alive and active. Sharper than any double-edged sword,
it penetrates even to dividing soul and spirit, joints and marrow;
it judges the thoughts and attitudes of the heart.
HEBREWS 4:12

FAMILY QUEST

Place three items on a table: a loaf of bread, a toy sword (a picture will do), and a flashlight. Say something like this: "Believe it or not, these three things have something in common: the Holy Bible. God's Word is described as 'our daily bread,' 'sharper than a sword,' and 'a light that guides our path.'"

TALK IT OUT

- How is the Bible like bread? (In other words, how is it like food that we eat every day?)
- How is the Word of God like a sword?
- How does scripture guide us on the right path—just like a flashlight? (If it's dark out, go outside with a flashlight.)

PARENT-CHILD CONNECTION

Tell your child that the Holy Bible is much more than a relic of an ancient religion or a collection of mere words printed on paper. It's unlike any other book ever written. Each chapter is packed with God's power. Explain that as we receive His message, it's as if the Lord's very breath of life is being breathed into us. Share these additional verses about scripture:

- "Heaven and earth will pass away, but my words will never pass away" (Luke 21:33).

- "We also have the prophetic message as something completely reliable, and you will do well to pay attention to it, as to a light shining in a dark place, until the day dawns and the morning star rises in your hearts. Above all, you must understand that no prophecy of Scripture came about by the prophet's own interpretation of things. For prophecy never had its origin in the human will, but prophets, though human, spoke from God as they were carried along by the Holy Spirit" (2 Peter 1:19–21).

TALK TO GOD

As you pray, encourage your child to (1) thank God for giving us the Bible so we can learn more about Him and (2) ask the Lord to help us read the Word daily.

BONUS TIPS:
TEN WAYS TO NURTURE SPIRITUAL GROWTH

TIP #1: BIBLE TEACHING BEGINS AT HOME

Just by reading these devotionals, you are showing you recognize how important it is to grow your family's faith. It is priority number one! So, congratulations. You're on the right track. Good job!

The family is the oldest and most basic of human and biblical institutions. The Bible stresses its importance as a training ground for mature adult character. The family is to be a community of teaching and learning about God and godliness, a place where children are instructed and encouraged to live their lives by the Word of God.

What the Bible says: Genesis 18:18–19; Deuteronomy 4:9; 6:6–8; 11:18–21; Proverbs 22:6; and Ephesians 6:4.

TIP #2: MAKE FAMILY DEVOTIONAL TIME A PRIORITY

Plan a specific time for family devotions if possible. This will make it part of your family's day and help you be consistent. Involve the whole family whenever you can.

Make Bible study experiential. As many parents discover, children begin learning through concrete and tangible processes: "Touch something hot; you feel pain." As they grow, their capacity for understanding more abstract concepts develops, allowing parents to begin teaching principles beyond mere cause and effect.

Use your Bible and teach your children how to use theirs.

Make family devotional time relaxed.

Change strategies if necessary. There are times, especially with young children, when you need to change strategies during a devotional time. Use this book as a guide to creatively engage your children and feel free to change it up when necessary.

TIP #3: KNOW THE KEYS TO SPIRITUAL GROWTH

How do we instill the values that are core to our faith?

How can we help our children nurture a genuine relationship with God when so many cultural voices are seeking to pull them away?

Here are three keys you can follow during each developmental stage of a child's life. Each can support your core Christian values as a family.

CREATE Relationship
CULTIVATE Character
Be CONSISTENT

TIP #4: DEVELOP A SPIRITUAL GROWTH STRATEGY

As parents, be intentional. Make a plan for your family's spiritual growth. Begin by asking some key questions:

*What are the core spiritual values we want to
    plant in the heart of our child?*
What kind of man or woman does God want our child to be?
*What do we sense God wants us to develop in
    our own walk with Christ?*
What faith lessons are we modeling for our child?

TIP #5: REMEMBER THAT CHILDREN SEE, CHILDREN DO

Your children learn what it means to be a Christian as they pattern their lives after yours, just as boys learn to be husbands and fathers by what they see you do, and little girls learn to be wives and mothers in the same way. Even the simple act of reading your Bible in front of your children can encourage them to make God's Word a priority.

Do you spend time with God every day in His Word? Make sure they know! In other words, "Preach often; and, if necessary, use words."

TIP #6: BEGIN BEFORE A CHILD IS BORN

It has been proven that unborn babies can hear and identify voices and sounds and can perceive light and dark. Consider this: while in the womb, John the Baptist leaped at the sound of Mary's voice and the presence of Jesus.

Many parents use the time during pregnancy to play music or sing worship songs to their unborn child. It is not unusual for those children to then respond with quietness or attentiveness to that same music after they are born. Praying for your unborn child out loud, calling them by name, and reading scripture to them creates a foundation for their relationship with God in the future.

TIP #7: REACH TODDLERS AND PRESCHOOLERS

Children are like little sponges during this time period. Building a strong foundation for their faith during this time creates a lasting impression and serves as a support throughout their lives.

This is the season of learning to relate to others, express oneself with words, comprehend language, walk for the first time, fall down and stand up again, sing, laugh, feed oneself, and distinguish pictures and colors.

Begin telling your child about God, Jesus, and the Holy Spirit. He won't understand the intangibles, but he will learn the names of God and they will become familiar to him. Teach him songs, sing and dance to Christian songs with him, point out the flowers, trees, sun, colors, and rainbows. As you teach him these words, explain how God created them.

TIP #8: REACH KIDS FROM KINDERGARTEN TO THIRD GRADE

Children in this age group are learning to sit still in a classroom and practice even greater self-control. They are subject to rules at school and now have the added responsibility of homework.

During this stage of a child's life, teaching God's love, acceptance, and justice helps her to recognize that there is a higher authority and a higher law. Children at this age begin to understand the concepts of fairness, mercy, justice, forgiveness, and loyalty, both in their relationship with you and in their relationship with God.

Telling your child Bible stories to illustrate biblical and spiritual principles will help her grasp these concepts. Having regular family worship times, reading the Bible together, praying, attending church together, and doing acts of service as a family teach your child through example about the importance of faith and living out your beliefs.

TIP #9: REACH KIDS FROM FOURTH GRADE TO SEVENTH GRADE

Children in this age group have real issues with self-identity, self-esteem, and acceptance. Cliques form and rejection by peers is a big issue. The Bible teaches that all people are valuable to God. Knowing they are loved by God and by you will go a long way in helping them develop and mature spiritually. Help your kids realize that God's Word has a lot to say about accepting every person, and He wants them to not only accept others but show them Jesus.

Excelling at school and meeting parental expectations are also challenges for this age group. A family culture that offers your kids affirmation and acceptance, balanced with healthy limits and discipline, can provide a safe place as they experience these significant challenges.

Spending time with your kids during this important season of life, tackling hard questions, addressing fears, discussing spiritual principles, and promoting their worth and value, will help ground them in truth and deepen your relationship with them.

TIP #10: REACH TEENAGERS

As we all know, the teenage years are a tumultuous time of hormones, identity crisis, relationships with the opposite sex, and struggles with self-expression. In addition, today's students live at home longer, go to college closer to home, and rely heavily on their parents' opinions and resources before making big decisions. This is the first generation of teens who actually watch less TV and live in "real time," getting most of their information through the use of social networking sites.

As you continue to worship as a family, ask your teenagers about their relationships with Jesus and be open to discussing any struggles they have, always sharing your own struggles with them. Begin to ask them their opinions, and be willing to be taught by them. Read a passage of scripture every day. Pray with them and over them and ask them to pray for you.

BONUS TIPS: THREE WAYS TO BOOST A TWEEN'S CONFIDENCE

Tweens need positive messages in order to build resilience and maintain an accurate portrait of who they are. In this stage they're between the periods of being entirely a child and entirely a teen. They're starting to want a sense of their own identity.

Here are some steps a parent would be wise to take:

Emphasize his innate worth. In as many ways as you can, communicate to him, "You are exactly who God created you to be, and very, very valuable—*just as you are.*"

Help her build an accurate and healthy identity. The proficient kids—athletically, academically, artistically, and so on—tend to be the ones who (seemingly) get all the attention, the ones held up by others as the standard for us all. God doesn't value gold medalists more or give special love to A+ students. Build into your child a sense of self that's biblically on target.

Establish together-time. Developmentally, children this age want to feel they're good at something, knowing that they can accomplish a task. It doesn't have to be every day, but strive to spend devoted time with your children. Special moments provide (1) a place of safety for kids and (2) an opportunity for Dad and Mom to speak encouraging words into their child's life.

" 'Together times' can also reinforce in children the sense that, 'Yeah, I can do this. I'm proficient at something; I can be a good soccer player. I'm a good friend,' " explains Dr. Trina Young-Greer.[1] She points out that